ACCURATE ENGLISH

LOWER INTERMEDIATE LEVEL

MICHAEL THORN

STUDENTS' BOOK 1

CASSELL

Cassell Publishers Ltd
Artillery House, Artillery Row, London SW1P 1RT

First published 1989
Reprinted (with corrections) 1990

Thorn, Michael
Accurate English.
Students' bk.1
1 English language, Questions & answers — For non—English speaking students
I. Title
428. 2'4

ISBN 0 304 31542 7

Accurate English consists of:
Students' Book 1   0 304 31542 7   Students' Book 2   0 304 315451
Practice Book 1   0 304 31543 5   Practice Book 2   0 304 31546 X
Teacher's Book 1   0 304 31544 3   Teacher's Book 2   0 304 31547 8
Cassettes 1 (2)   0 304 31548 6   Cassettes 2 (2)   0 304 31549 4

Editorial and Design Management by Apollo Publishing
Illustrations by Michael Bettney
Typeset by Trendsetters
Printed and bound in Spain by Graficas Reunidas, Madrid

Photographs in this publication were kindly provided by the following sources:

Alfred Marks; Barclays Bank plc; BBC Photographic Library; British Airways; Driving Instructors' Association; Eastbourne Borough Council; Harrods Ltd; HM Prison Service; Sotheby's (London); The Maritime Trust; Thomson Citybreaks; Trustees of the Science Museum (London).

TO THE STUDENTS

Learning a foreign language is never easy, but the more you know, the more interesting it becomes. People learn languages for different reasons. Sometimes they need to **speak** the language in the course of their work, other times they need to read and understand written texts. Then again, sadly, some people learn a language just in order to pass an exam.

I remember learning French and German for this reason at school. I passed both the examinations, but I didn't **really** begin to learn either language until later, when I had a chance to visit France and Germany. Then I realised how much more fun it is to visit a country when you can speak and understand the language, even if you don't do either perfectly. Just to be able to order your first cup of coffee in a foreign country, speaking **their** language, makes you feel great — a citizen of the world.

So I hope this book will help **you** to improve your English. You're lucky, in a way, because so many people all over the world speak English that wherever you go there is a chance that you will make new friends.

Good luck with your studies.

Michael Thorn

Contents

FUNCTIONS	LISTENING
Talking about habits; asking about habits	An interview with a postman
Talking about past events; asking about past events	A radio news bulletin
Asking questions; expressing negative thoughts	An interview with a woman who bought a painting
Talking about things that are happening now	A newsflash about a fire at a cinema
Talking about future events	A schoolboy talking about his essay prize
Talking about physical appearances of things; talking about people's characters	Radio advertisements
Saying how people did things and how things happened	Tips on how to approach an interview
Saying when things happened	Three young people meet after five years
Talking about intentions; making predictions	Young people talking about their ambitions
Talking about experiences; asking about a mutual acquaintance	Telephone conversation between a young man and his sister
Giving reasons for things; saying what people have been doing	Telephone conversation about a couple's new flat
Comparing people and things	Extract from a broadcast about learning English
Comparing people and things	An interview with a television news reporter
Talking about preferences giving advice; asking for and giving permission	Radio phone-in programme — the radio doctor
Saying when things happened	Radio account of an industrial dispute
Expressing possibilities; making suggestions; expressing preferences	A conversation between two young people in a cafe
Making predictions; stating decisions that have been taken	A radio advertisement aimed to persuade young people to open a bank account
Talking about obligations making recommendations	A radio discussion about body building
Describing things that happened in detail	An interview with the captain of a fishing boat
Giving advice; asking hypothetical questions	Extract from a radio programme about buying and selling property

THE SECRET DREAM

Reading

A WHAT CRITICISMS DO PEOPLE MAKE OF CONCORDE?

I work in a small office from 9.0 till 5.0 Monday to Friday. Occasionally my boss asks me to come in on a Saturday morning as well. I don't earn a large salary and my job is rather dull, really. But I have a secret dream. My dream is to make a return flight to New York on Concorde. I know people say rude things about it. They say that it's noisy and expensive and that it uses too much fuel, and that it doesn't really carry enough passengers.

Yet every time Concorde passes overhead, people stop in the street and stare up at it, simply because it's so beautiful. This happens all over the world, so it's not just me that's crazy. There must be something a bit special about it.

My problem is that I can only afford to put aside £5 a week and a return ticket to New York costs over £1000. Then of course New York is quite an expensive city, they say.

Never mind. The photograph of Concorde over my desk always cheers me up. One day, perhaps . . .

COMPREHENSION QUESTIONS

1 What happens when Concorde flies over?
2 Why do you think people react like this?
3 Do you ever see Concorde pass overhead?
4 How much is the writer able to save each week?
5 What effect does the photo of Concorde have on the writer?

Exercise

B WORD BUILDING

You may use a dictionary for this exercise. Write out this short description of what takes place when a passenger arrives at an airport, putting in the missing words and phrases from the list below:

flight number – check in desk – weight limit – departure lounge – one piece of hand baggage – boarding pass – labels – passport control – duty free shop – baggage.

When the passenger arrives at the airport, he takes his ____1____ to the ____2____. Sometimes there is a ____3____ so the suitcases must be weighed. Then the airline official ties ____4____ onto them and gives the passenger a ____5____. He then goes through ____6____ to the ____7____. Sometimes he visits the ____8____. Then he waits until his ____9____ is called. Usually he is only allowed to take ____10____ onto the plane.

C PRACTISE ASKING QUESTIONS. BELOW ARE THE ANSWERS TO SOME QUESTIONS ABOUT THE TEXT.

▷ *Example: He works in a small office.*
          Where . . . ?
           Q: Where does the writer work?
           A: He works in a small office.

1 What . . . ?
  He starts work at 9 o'clock.
2 When . . . ?
  At 5 o'clock.
3 . . . ever . . . on a Saturday?
  Yes, he sometimes works on a Saturday.
4 . . . much money?
  No, he doesn't earn a lot of money.
5 . . . very interesting?
  No, it's rather boring.
6 . . . want to do?
  To fly across the Atlantic in Concorde.
7 . . . Concorde . . . very fast?
  Yes, very.
8 How much . . . ?
  Over £1000.

D WORK IN PAIRS. HAVE CONVERSATIONS LIKE THIS:

A: Does a dentist cut men's hair?
B: No, he doesn't. He looks after people's teeth.

1 A butcher 2 A barber 3 A baker 4 A carpenter
5 A plumber 6 A nurse 7 A mechanic 8 A waiter
9 A pilot 10 A detective

E CONTINUE TO WORK IN PAIRS. ASK AND ANSWER QUESTIONS BEGINNING WITH <u>WHERE</u>, <u>WHAT</u>, AND <u>DO</u>, LIKE THIS:

▷ *Example: When/go/bed?*
          Q: When do you go to bed?
          A: About 11 o'clock.

1 Where/live?
2 What/have/breakfast?
3 When/get up?
4 Where/go/for your holidays?
5 Do/go home/lunch?
6 What/eat/lunch?

UNIT
1

F CONTINUE TO DISCUSS YOUR OWN HABITS. ASK ANOTHER STUDENT IN THE CLASS QUESTIONS USING:

ADVERBS OF FREQUENCY:

always, **usually**, **often**, **sometimes**, **occasionally**, or **never**.

▷ _Example: chocolate_
       Q: Do you ever eat chocolate?
       A: Yes, I often eat chocolate.

1 chocolate	6 the cinema
2 tea	7 football
3 bicycle	8 discos
4 television	9 by train
5 the radio	10 photographs

NOTE HOW WE FORM THE SIMPLE PRESENT.

Statements:

I / You	start	early in the morning.
He/She/It	starts	
We / You / They	start	

Negatives:

I / You	don't		
He/She/It	doesn't	start	early in the morning.
We / You / They	don't		

Questions:

Do	I / you		
Does	he/she/it	start	early in the morning?
Do	we / you / they		

Wh . . ? questions:

Where	do	I/you	work?
When	does	he/she/it	work with?
Who	do	we/you/they	

SPECIAL POINTS TO NOTE

You will find that the Simple Present tense is useful when you want to talk about things that
a   happen regularly (or never)
b   are (or aren't) always true

▷ *Examples: What does Robert do?*
He works in an office.
He doesn't work in a shop.

We often use the Simple Present tense with adverbs of frequency like:
always, usually, often, sometimes, occasionally, never.

▷ *Examples: Robert sometimes takes the children to the park.*
His wife usually buys the groceries at the supermarket.
Robert never drives very fast.

G LISTENING

AN EARLY START

You are going to hear a woman asking Tom some questions about his job. Before you listen to the tape, study the following vocabulary:

sort the letters: put the letters in the correct order
deliver: take to someone's house
rubber band: thin piece of rubber used for keeping things together

Listen to this interview with a postman called Tom, several times if necessary. Then decide whether the following statements are true or false.

1 Tom leaves home at 5 o'clock in the morning.
2 The first thing Tom does is deliver the letters.
3 Tom puts a rubber band round each letter.
4 Tom has a cup of coffee about 10 o'clock in the morning.
5 Tom sometimes delivers more than one lot of letters at Christmas time.

Listen again to the interview, more than once if necessary, and write down the sentences in which Tom uses each of the following words:

6 always
7 sometimes
8 often
9 occasionally
10 usually
11 never

Writing

H WRITING ACTIVITY

PUNCTUATION

We always begin a sentence in English with a capital letter. We also use capital letters for people's names, the names of countries, nationalities, the days of the week and the months. We finish a sentence with a full stop.

▷ *Examples: Tom is an English postman. He never works on Sunday.*

Copy out the text below, putting in capital letters and full stops where necessary:

tom works for the post office every morning he gets up early he has his breakfast and then he goes to the post office first he sorts his letters after that he leaves the post office and delivers the letters every day tom has some letters to take to a big house it is a school where young people come to learn english there are often some letters with spanish or italian stamps on them sometimes there are letters from as far away as japan

SOMETIMES IT PAYS TO ARGUE

Reading

A WHICH SPORT DOES FATIMA WHITBREAD TAKE PART IN? WHY WAS 1986 AN IMPORTANT YEAR IN HER LIFE?

Fatima Whitbread lived in children's homes until she was 13 because her mother, who came from Cyprus, was unable to look after her.

When Fatima was 12 she took part in a game of netball. The referee, whose name was Margaret Whitbread, noticed the young girl because she argued with so many of her decisions. A few weeks later they met again at a local sports ground. Fatima asked Margaret to show her how to throw the javelin and Margaret soon discovered that although Fatima was a difficult child, she was a very promising young athlete.

Margaret was married and had two sons. One day one of the boys said: 'We'd like Fatima as a big sister'. Eventually, when she was 13, the Whitbreads adopted her.

Family life suited Fatima and as she became bigger and stronger, her javelin throwing improved until she became one of Britain's top athletes. She had her ups and downs and she missed the Los Angeles Olympics through injury. But in August 1986, at the European championships, which took place at Stuttgart, in Germany, she set a new world record with a huge throw of 77.44 metres.

'This heals a lot of wounds', she said.

UNIT

2

Work in pairs. Practise asking questions in the past and replying with short answers. Like this:

Ask where Fatima's mother came from.
Where did Fatima's mother come from?
From Cyprus.

1 Ask why Fatima spent so much time in children's homes.
2 Ask why the referee noticed Fatima.
3 Ask where Fatima met Margaret again.
4 Ask what Margaret showed Fatima.
5 Ask what the Whitbreads did when Fatima was 13.
6 Ask why Fatima missed the Los Angeles Olympics.
7 Ask where the European championships took place in 1986.
8 Ask how far Fatima threw the javelin in Stuttgart.

B WORD BUILDING

Match the names of the following sports with the aims listed below.

▷ *Example: Javelin.*
          You have to throw the javelin as far as possible.

American football – boxing – football – high jump – hockey – long jump – marathon – snooker – tennis – weight lifting

1 Kick the ball into your opponent's net.
2 Score a touchdown.
3 Jump over the bar.
4 Punch your opponent more often than he punches you.
5 Hit the ball over the net.
6 Jump as far as possible.
7 Run a very long way as fast as possible.
8 Hit the ball into your opponent's goal.
9 Lift heavy weights.
10 Pot all the balls.

C MANY COMMON VERBS HAVE IRREGULAR PAST FORMS. THE FOLLOWING WERE USED IN THE PASSAGE:

▷ *Example: become – became, come – came, meet – met,*
          set – set, take – took, throw – threw.

HERE ARE 12 MORE:

bite – bit, catch – caught, fly – flew, hear – heard, hide – hid, lie – lay, ride – rode, shoot – shot, spill – spilt, stick – stuck, think – thought, wear – wore.

UNIT

2

Work in pairs. Make sure you know the meaning of all these verbs. Then use some of them to provide suitable answers to the following questions:

1 What did the thief do with the stolen silver?
2 How did the eagle reach its nest?
3 Why was there milk all over the floor?
4 What did the guard dog do to the postman?
5 What did the people do when the gunman started shooting?
6 Why did Stella break off her engagement to Paul?
7 Why did the old lady draw back the curtain and look out into the night?
8 What happened to the little boy who got superglue all over his fingers?
9 What did Alfred do when he found that the grey suit was too small for him?
10 What did the cowboy do when the lady refused to marry him?

Exercise

D WE USE THE SIMPLE PAST FOR ANY ACTION THAT TOOK PLACE AT A DEFINITE POINT OF TIME IN THE PAST. BELOW ARE TEN EXAMPLES OF POINTS OF TIME IN THE PAST.

Think of ten things that happened, one for each point of time.

▷ *Example: on Tuesday*
   George came to see me on Tuesday.

1 on Sunday
2 at 2 o'clock
3 last week
4 in 1981
5 six months ago

6 yesterday
7 this morning
8 in August
9 an hour ago
10 last night

Exercise

E STUDY THE HEADLINES BELOW:

JANUARY
POLICE ARREST FAMOUS RACING DRIVER

SEPTEMBER
FAMOUS ACTOR DIES ON STAGE

MARCH
LIGHT PLANE CRASHES ON SAN FRANCISCO HOTEL

Write a sentence for each headline explaining what happened.

▷ *Example: In January police arrested a famous racing driver.*

Then work in pairs. Think of a dozen interesting/dramatic events, one for each month of last year. Write one sentence saying what happened in each case.

Your headlines may refer to things that really happened or to imaginary events.

NOTE HOW WE FORM THE SIMPLE PAST.

Statements:

I You etc	saw	that film last night.

Negatives:

I You etc.	did not (didn't)	see	that film last night.

Questions:

Did	I you etc	see	that film last night?

Where When How	did	you	go?

The past of many verbs is formed by adding -d or -ed

▷ *Examples: live — lived*
notice — noticed
discover — discovered

But we form the past of many other verbs by changing the spelling in various ways.

▷ *Examples: catch — caught, come — came, do — did, is — was, were, have — had, take — took, throw — threw, wear — wore.*

You will find a list of all the most important irregular verbs at the back of this book. Use the list for reference and learn the forms carefully a few at a time.

UNIT
2

SPECIAL POINTS TO NOTE

The Simple Past is used to described an action that took place at a definite **point of time** in the past.

▷ *Examples:* **She took part** in a game of netball **when she was 12.**
She set a new world record **in August 1986.**

'When did the dog bite the postman?'
'Last week'.
'How terrible!'
'Yes, the postman was furious'.

Note. We must say — the postman was furious — because we are referring to something that happened last week.

Often the point of time in the past is understood, but not stated. Look at some more examples:

Where did you buy those shoes? (When you went shopping.)
I had a chat with Peter. (When I met him this morning.)

Here are some more examples of points of time:

yesterday — on Friday — in 1985 — this morning (probably used in the afternoon or in the evening) — last month — when I was young

We also use the Simple Past tense with the expression ago. You will have more practice using ago in unit 8.

F LISTENING

NEWS OF THE DAY

You are going to hear a radio news bulletin. Before you listen to the tape, study the following vocabulary:

interpreter:	person who translates what someone says into another language.
White House:	official home of the American President
spokesman:	person who speaks officially
arms:	weapons
frank:	open and honest
lorries:	trucks
dye:	colour that doesn't wash out
mechanical fault:	problem with the engine
explosion:	loud noise (as when a bomb goes off)
test:	examination
fuss:	unnecessary excitement

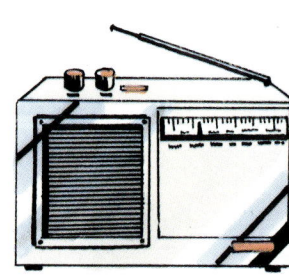

Listen to the tape, several times if necessary, then answer the questions below.

1 Who met and what did they talk about?
2 What did the Soviet television reporter say about the meeting?
3 What were James Godber's thoughts about the meeting?
4 What did the French farmers do? Why did they take this action?
5 Jack Thompson took his dog for a walk in the park, but he got a surprise. Explain what happened.
6 It was a good day for Leonard Dimmock. Why?
7 Do you think he was surprised? Explain why/why not.

G WRITING ACTIVITY

PUTTING SENTENCES IN ORDER

During the Listening Activity you heard some news stories. Here is another news story that appeared in a local newspaper. But the sentences are printed in the wrong order. Write out the story, putting the sentences in the correct order:

A GOLDEN DISCOVERY

It was old and in very bad condition.
'That certainly was a good buy,' said Mr Frost.
Mr Frost, who lives in Perry Hill, likes buying old furniture and restoring* it.
Mr Frost brought the chair home in the back of his car.
Suddenly a number of gold coins fell out onto the grass.
He put it in his cellar and forgot all about it.
Mr Frost took them to a local jeweller who valued them at over £400.
He took it into the garden and began to remove the old cover.
Last summer he went to Worthing for the day and bought a small armchair for £5.

*putting it in good condition again.

17

UNIT
2

I WANT YOU TO DRAW A TREE

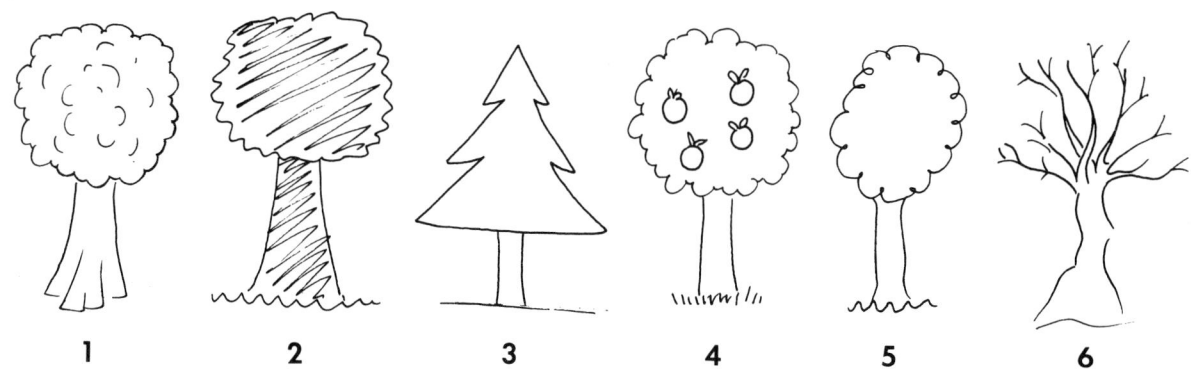

1   2   3   4   5   6

Reading

A WHAT CAN A DRAWING OF A TREE TELL YOU?

Some people believe that the kind of tree you draw shows what kind of person you are. So we asked a number of people to draw a tree.

A lot of people drew tree number I. People who drew a tree like this are sensible and affectionate. They aren't aggressive and they often have little ambition.

Many people also drew number 5. People who drew this tree are self-disciplined and able to keep their feelings under control. They are not afraid to think for themselves.

A few people drew tree number 4, a fruit tree. People who drew this sort of tree like being the centre of attention. They have a strong sense of drama and are good at telling stories.

A very small number of people drew tree number 3. People who drew this tree have a strong personality and they aren't at all patient with anybody they think is being stupid. They can be very sarcastic.

A few people also drew tree number 6. Those who drew this tree are difficult to work with because they are always criticising their friends and colleagues.

Nobody drew tree number 2. This is a good thing because people who drew trees like this usually feel lonely and isolated. They are shy and find it difficult to make friends.

Personally I'm not sure there's much truth in all this. What do you think?

UNIT

3

ORAL QUESTIONS

1 What did the writer ask people to do?
2 How many people drew tree number 1?
3 What can we say about the people who drew this sort of tree?
4 Did many people draw tree number 5?
5 What can we say about these people's character?
6 Which tree did very impatient people with a strong personality draw?
7 What can we say about the people who drew a fruit tree?
8 How many people drew a fruit tree?
9 Why are the people who drew tree number 6 difficult to work with?
10 How many people drew tree number 2?

B WORD BUILDING

Fill in the crossword. All the words are connected with the garden and growing things.

Across

1 Grapes grow on this.
4 This insect makes honey.
5 A fruit.
7 Thickest part of a tree.
8 They are small and hard and usually grow on trees. We can eat them.
10 A new plant grows from this.
12 Florists sell these.
14 Another name for 2 down.
15 Used to protect fruit trees from the birds.

Down

1 Carrots and potatoes are _____.
2 Plants grow in this.
3 Birds do this when eating.
4 Part of a tree.
6 To cut back trees or roses.
9 We _____ 10 across to grow food.
11 What you do with a spade.
13 It warms the garden.

UNIT

3

C WE SAY: HOW MUCH TIME HAVE WE GOT?
HOW MANY LETTERS DID YOU WRITE?

Below are the answers to 10 questions, beginning with **How much** or **How many**. Work in pairs and think of suitable questions.

1 How . . . ?
I paid £40.
2 How . . . ?
We invited more than 50 people.
3 How . . . ?
I bought half a pound.
4 How . . . ?
I have four letters to post.
5 How . . .?
He charged me £4, but he did a very good job.
6 How . . . ?
She's got three. Two go to school and then there's the baby.
7 How . . . ?
I need enough to make a pullover.
8 How . . . ?
Too much, I'm afraid. It's terribly salty, isn't it?
9 How . . . ?
Eighteen is the maximum, but we try to keep our classes as small as possible.
10 How . . . ?
I used one complete roll of film . . . that's 24 photographs.

D STUDY THESE CONVERSATIONS:

Sue: How much petrol did you put in the tank?
Pete: I only put in **a little**. or I put in **a lot.**

Pete: How many biscuits did you eat?
Sue: I only ate **a few**. or I ate **a lot**.

Work in pairs. Use the nouns below to make similar conversations.

1 coffee	5 time	8 tickets
2 sandwiches	6 games	9 information
3 cake	7 money	10 fruit
4 stamps		

E WE SAY: THEY STOLE SOME MONEY.
DID ANYBODY SEE THE THIEF?
WE DIDN'T SEE ANYTHING.

Use <u>some</u>, <u>somebody</u>, <u>something</u>, <u>any</u>, <u>anybody</u>, or <u>anything</u> to complete the following sentences.

1 Does _____ know where the station is?
2 I lent that cassette to _____, but I can't remember who.
3 After the accident he couldn't remember _____.
4 We didn't buy _____ apples.
5 Oh yes. There is _____ I wanted to say to you.

UNIT
3

6 Isn't there _____ we can do to help?

7 There were _____ very pretty tunes in the show.

8 She didn't say _____ about her husband.

9 I'm sure _____ told the police about it.

10 Vegetarians don't eat _____ meat at all.

F WE CAN EXPRESS A NEGATIVE THOUGHT IN TWO DIFFERENT WAYS:

There **wasn't anybody** at the reception desk.
There **was nobody** at the reception desk.

Turn the following **not . . . any** negatives into **no** negatives.
Use **no**, **nobody**, or **nothing**.

1 I don't know anybody at this party.
2 I can't tell you anything about it.
3 I didn't have any money with me.
4 There wasn't anything I could do.
5 There isn't any time for me to explain now.
6 I couldn't see anything.
7 There isn't any point in arguing about it.
8 I'm afraid I haven't got any change on me.
9 They didn't do anything about it.
10 They didn't have any cheese at the shop.

G IDEA FOR DISCUSSION

The class should divide into two groups of three or four. Without looking again at the sketches of trees in the book, each draw a tree of your own. Then compare your tree with those illustrated.

Talk about your drawings and the personalities of the people in your group. Do you find any connection between people's drawings and their character? Or is the whole idea nonsense?

SPECIAL POINTS TO NOTE

We use **some**, **somebody** or **someone**, **something** when expressing affirmative ideas:

> Look, I can see **some** pretty china plates over there.
> I lent **somebody** my torch and I never got it back.
> There was definitely **something** strange about Higgins.

We use **any**, **anybody** or **anyone**, **anything** when expressing negative ideas:

> There isn't **any** coffee in the pot.
> Don't tell **anyone** yet.
> I'm afraid I can't do **anything** about it.

and asking questions:

> Is there **any** coffee in the pot?
> Did I tell **anybody** else about this?
> Can't you do **anything** to help?

Exercise

Exercise

We use <u>no</u>, <u>nobody</u> or <u>no one</u> to express negative ideas in a particularly strong way:

> There is **no** time to waste.
> **No one** noticed that the brooch was missing.
> There is absolutely **nothing** I can do.

We use <u>how many</u> and <u>a few</u> with nouns we can count:

> **How many** invitations did you send?
> I got rid of **a few** old books last week.

and *how much* and *a little* with nouns we can't count.
> **How much** milk do you want in your tea?
> I can lend you **a little** money if necessary.

We use <u>a lot of</u> with both countables and uncountables

> I saw **a lot of** old friends at the party.
> I've spent **a lot of** time on this job.

H LISTENING

Listening

A GENUINE BARGAIN

You are going to hear an interview with a woman who bought a painting.
Before you listen to the tape, study the following vocabulary:

valuable:	worth a lot of money
Renoir:	famous French painter
auction:	type of sale where the person who offers the highest price gets the article being sold
porcelain:	china
takes my fancy:	I like
experienced auction goer:	person who often goes to auction sales
set myself a limit of £10:	made a decision not to pay more than £10
bid:	offered
frame:	border (around picture or mirror)
bargains:	articles being sold very cheaply

Listen to the tape, then answer the following questions:

 1 Why is Rosemary on the programme?
 2 How much did she pay?
 3 How much does Rosemary know about art?
 4 How much is the painting worth?
 5 Why did she buy the painting?

6 Does Rosemary buy many things at auction sales?
7 What sort of things does she usually buy?
8 Did Rosemary bid for the painting herself?
9 How much did she intend to pay?
10 What does Rosemary think of the frame?
11 What did Rosemary think her husband might do?
12 How did Rosemary feel when she learnt that the
    painting was valuable?

Writing

I WRITING ACTIVITY

PUNCTUATION

We use a comma to separate different parts of a sentence and so help the reader to understand the writer's exact meaning.

Below is printed an extract from an article about money. Re-write the article, putting in capital letters, full stops and commas where necessary.

in a recent broadcast i heard a woman say that she felt guilty because she spent £20 at an auction sale she was afraid her husband might accuse her of being extravagant i find this attitude difficult to understand for obviously a married woman has as much right to spend £20 as her husband sometimes both husband and wife go out to work but in a case where the woman stays at home to look after the children perhaps it is unfair that she should feel guilty about spending a small sum of money on herself.

Reading

A WHICH TOWN DOES THIS PASSAGE DESCRIBE?

It is November and the passengers on the commuter train coming into the city are wearing their scarves and overcoats.
A grey mist hangs over the river and the scene reminds me of Monet's famous painting of the Thames below Westminster.

Near Buckingham Palace the pavements are damp and leaves are still falling from the trees. Nobody is feeding the pigeons in Trafalgar Square any more and there are fewer visitors to the National Gallery than there were last week. Outside Charing Cross station an old man is selling poppies, for next Sunday is Remembrance Day.

At the bottom of Whitehall, near the Houses of Parliament, workmen are digging a large hole in the road. This hole is causing a traffic jam which stretches back as far as the eye can see. By half past four it is already getting dark. The buses are all lit up inside and the cars and taxis have their headlights on. What are all those drivers thinking about, I wonder, as they sit there so patiently waiting for the traffic lights to change?

UNIT
4

COMPREHENSION QUESTIONS

1 Is it winter or summer?
2 What are the commuters wearing?
3 What did Monet do?
4 Why are the pavements probably slippery?
5 Why are the pigeons in Trafalgar Square unhappy?
6 What is the old man outside Charing Cross station doing?
7 What are the workmen doing?
8 What usually happens when workmen do this?
9 Why do all the cars have their headlights on by 4 p.m.?
10 What happens when the traffic lights turn green?

B WORD BUILDING

Exercise

Study these 10 words and phrases used in describing weather conditions, then match them with the definitions below:

breeze – cloudy – dew – frost – gale – hail – lightning – mist – snow – thunder

1 Strong wind.
2 Gentle wind.
3 Flashes of light in the sky.
4 Frozen drops of rain.
5 Small drops of water which form on grass etc. on cold nights.
6 Loud noise in the sky during storms.
7 Frozen state of the air and the ground when the temperature falls below freezing.
8 Thin fog.
9 Small soft white pieces of frozen water that fall from the sky.
10 It's this when the sun is hidden behind the clouds.

UNIT

4

Exercise

C LOOK AT THE TWO PICTURES OF A SCENE AT A RAILWAY STATION. WORK IN PAIRS. FIND 12 DIFFERENCES BETWEEN THE TWO PICTURES AND WRITE A SENTENCE DESCRIBING EACH OF THESE DIFFERENCES. USE TWO COLUMNS LIKE THIS:

IN PICTURE ONE

The man sitting on the seat is reading a book.

Continue in the same way.

IN PICTURE TWO

He's reading a newspaper.

Exercise ▷

D PRACTISE USING THE SIMPLE PRESENT AND THE PRESENT CONTINUOUS TENSES.

Example: This man is a professional footballer.
What's he doing? He's kicking a football.
What other other things do professional footballers do?
They give interviews.
They make television advertisements.
They train several times a week.

1 This man is a vet.
What's he doing?
What other things do vets do?

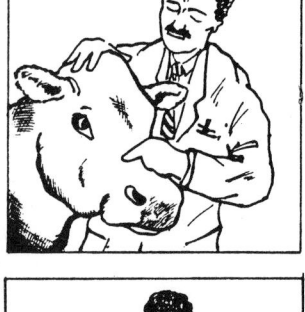

2 This man is a b . . . .
What's he doing?
What other things do b . . . s do?

3 This woman is an antique dealer.
What's she doing?
How do antique dealers make their money?

4 This man is a c . . . .
What's he doing?
Think of some of the things that c . . . s make.

5 This man is an a . . . .
What's he doing?
What other things do a . . . s do?

6 This man is a m . . . .
What's he doing?
What do m . . . s do?

UNIT
4

26

7 This man is an architect.
What's he doing?
What do a . . . s do?

8 This man is a b . . . .
What's he doing?
What other things do b . . . s do?

9 This girl is a s . . . .
What's she doing?
What other things do s . . . s do?

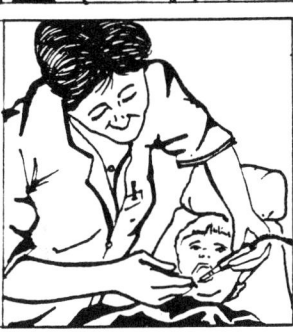

10 This woman is a d . . . .
What's she doing?
What other things do d . . . s do?

NOTE HOW WE FORM THE PRESENT CONTINUOUS

Statements:

I	am	
You	are	
He/She/It	is	waiting for her.
We You They	are	

Negatives:

I	am	
You	are	
He/She/It	is	not waiting for her.
We You They	are	

Questions:

Am	I	
Are	you	
Is	he/she/it	waiting for her?
Are	We you they	

▷ Note that contractions are often used.

Examples: I'm, I'm not, he's, he isn't, they aren't.

Such contractions are really a reproduction of spoken language.

UNIT
4

SPECIAL POINTS TO NOTE

Students sometimes confuse the use of the Present Continuous and the Simple Present. Remember that we use the Present Continuous for an action that is or isn't taking place, at the moment the speaker is speaking.

▷ Examples: *What is happening now?*
Smoke is coming from the upstairs window.
I'm afraid this clock isn't working.

The Present Continuous is also used when talking about future events. (See unit 5).

We use the Simple Present to describe actions which take place regularly.

▷ Example: *The postman delivers letters every day except Sunday.*

and for things which are always, or never, true.

▷ Example: *Hens lay eggs.*
Hens don't usually fly.

E LISTENING

FILMS AND FLAMES

You are going to hear a newsflash about a fire at a cinema.
Before you listen to the tape study the following vocabulary:

scene:	place where it happened
apparently:	it seems
screen:	big white or silver surface where the people see the picture
projectionist:	man or woman who shows the film
stalls:	the seats downstairs in the cinema
material:	cloth, plastic, etc
flashed:	showed
affected:	troubled
exit:	place where people leave
a fair bit:	quite a lot
ribs:	curved bones that go from your backbone to your chest
sightseers:	people who want to see what is happening
burst through:	come through suddenly
ambulance:	vehicle used to take sick or injured people to hospital

Listen to this radio newsflash about a fire at a cinema.
Then answer these questions as accurately as you can:

1 Where did the fire start?
2 What caused the fire?

3 How did the projectionist first become aware of the fire?

4 Why didn't the curtain burn quickly?

5 What did the projectionist do when he realised there was a fire?

6 Describe how the people left the cinema.

Listen to the tape again, more than once if necessary. Below are the answers to a number of questions. You write the questions. The prompts will help you.

▷ *Example: Q: Is anybody inside the building?*
A: No, there isn't anybody still inside the building.

7 . . . police . . ?
They are keeping sightseers away from the front of the building.

8 . . . fire officers . . ?
They are trying to put the fire out.

9 . . . the black smoke . . ?
It's coming out of the upstairs windows and the hole in the roof.

10 . . . the fire officer with the hose . . ?
He's standing at the very top of a tall ladder.

11 . . . ambulances . . ?
They're taking injured people to the hospital.

12 . . . suffering from . . ?
A few of them have broken bones, but most of them are having breathing problems caused by the smoke.

Writing

F WRITING ACTIVITY

USING THE PRESENT

Write a short description of the scene in the photograph. Describe the weather, the people and say what they are doing. Use about 150 words.

UNIT
4

Reading

A

14, Old School Lane,
Lingfield
Surrey
15th June

Dear Pierre,

Thank you for your letter. I'm glad you liked the photos. You must send me one of your little sister. I wonder if she still remembers me?

You're right about examinations. I took four this week and I'm taking chemistry and biology next week. Then, the week after, the holidays begin. Thank goodness!

The book you sent me is very interesting — I'm about half way through. I think Simenon writes well, but I'm afraid I still read French terribly slowly. Never mind. We're going to France for a few days during the holiday. Practice makes perfect, they say.

Unfortunately we aren't coming anywhere near Paris. My father can only get a few days off work and as he doesn't really like driving on the right, we're not taking the car. We're staying at a small hotel in Dinan, a pleasant little town on the river Rance. We stayed there once before. We're not planning to do anything very ambitious; see a bit of Britanny, take a few photographs and enjoy some good French food. I hope to persuade the family to spend one day at Mont St Michel. It's not far from Dinan and I believe it's really worth seeing.

As I say, we're only staying a few days in France. Then I'm going to Cornwall to spend three weeks with my Aunt Lucie. You met her once when you came to stay. Do you remember?

Write soon so that I get your letter before we leave for France.

Love from all the family,

Alice.

COMPREHENSION QUESTIONS

1 Who is the letter from?
2 Where does Pierre live?
3 How do you know that Alice once met Pierre's sister?
4 What book is Alice reading?
5 Why is she reading it slowly?
6 What is the Rance?
7 Is Alice sure she's going to visit Mont St Michel? Explain why/why not.
8 Where does Aunt Lucie live?

Exercise

B WORD BUILDING

Below is a short list of things we might do on holiday. Work in pairs and agree on an order, with your **favourite** activity at the top of the list and the activity you enjoy least at the bottom. If you can't agree, you'll have to compromise.

sunbathing – walking – exploring ancient cities – swimming – playing games – taking part in water sports – sailing – visiting museums and art galleries – meeting new friends – discovering unusual dishes

When you have made your list, compare it with the lists of students sitting near you.

Exercise

C HERE ARE THE ANSWERS TO A NUMBER OF QUESTIONS ABOUT THE TEXT. WHAT WERE THE QUESTIONS?

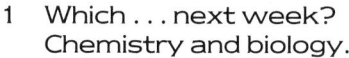

Example: How many . . . next week?
How many exams is Alice taking next week?
Two.

1 Which . . . next week?
Chemistry and biology.

2 Why . . . they . . . the car?
Because Alice's father doesn't like driving on the right.

3 Why . . . they . . . to Paris?
Alice's father can only get a few days off work.

4 Which part . . . to?
To Britanny.

5 Where . . . ?
At a small hotel in Dinan.

6 What . . . during their holiday?
Nothing very ambitious.

7 How long . . . in France?
Only for a few days, unfortunately.

8 Where . . . Alice . . . after they get back from France?
To visit her aunt in Cornwall.

Exercise

D WORK IN PAIRS. MAKE 10 DIALOGUES BY COMBINING ONE REMARK FROM COLUMN 1 WITH ONE FROM COLUMN 2 AND ONE FROM COLUMN 3. USE EACH REMARK ONCE ONLY.

When you have completed your 10 dialogues you will have **two** extra remarks left over from column 1. Add two more exchanges to each of these to complete dialogues 11 and 12.

Then choose any **one** of the completed dialogues and expand it into an interesting conversation by adding 5 to 10 further exchanges.

	COLUMN 1	COLUMN 2	COLUMN 3
1	Is it true that Tom's leaving the firm?	The people downstairs are terribly noisy.	Just a small operation.
2	I'm going into hospital next week.	About £30, I believe. Why?	Let's hope they can keep up the repayments.
3	Where are you planning to stay in the USA?	She says she has too much work to do.	Really? What a shame.
4	Why is the baker's shop closing down?	I enjoyed it.	She works awfully hard, doesn't she?
5	When are you getting your photos back?	Yes, he feels it's time he moved on.	We're going on Saturday.
6	How are George and Annie paying for the new car?	Oh, I hope it's nothing serious?	I'm looking forward to seeing them.
7	Why is he learning Russian?	Too few customers, I believe.	I'm thinking of changing my job too.
8	What did you think of the film?	On Friday, I hope.	That sounds exciting.
9	How much was that radio?	I believe they're getting a loan from the bank.	Oh, then I don't blame you.
10	Why are you leaving your flat?	To Kenya.	I'm thinking of buying one myself.
11	Why isn't Emma coming to the party?		
12	Where are you going for your holiday?		

SPECIAL POINTS TO NOTE

The forms for the Present Continuous used to express the future are exactly the same as those used for the ordinary Present Continuous tense. (See unit 4).

When we use the Present Continuous to talk about future events, we are usually talking about something which we are **sure** will happen.

UNIT 5

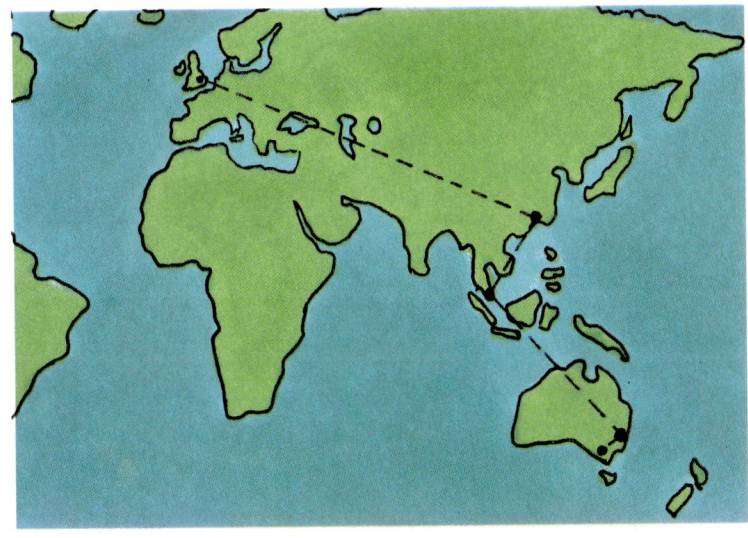

Examples: *I'm seeing him tomorrow morning. (The speaker has an appointment)*
We're flying Pan American. (They paid for their tickets)
Mike and Sheila aren't coming to the party. (They replied to the invitation regretting that they could not come).

Exercise

E LISTENING

THE JOURNEY OF A LIFETIME

You are going to hear a schoolboy talking about his success in a competition. Before you listen to the tape study the following vocabulary:

essay:	written composition
journey:	trip
keen:	enthusiastic
editor:	person responsible for deciding what is published in a newspaper or magazine
imaginary:	not real
research:	study of a subject
set:	placed

Listen, several times if necessary, to this radio interview with Peter Parker. Then decide whether the following statements are true or false.

1 Peter won a writing competition.
2 He is a schoolboy.
3 Peter is also the editor of a fashion magazine.
4 Peter wrote the story of a trip he made across the United States.
5 He got some of his ideas from films.
6 Peter is travelling to Hong Kong by air.
7 He is staying at a hotel near the harbour.
8 Peter doesn't really want to go to Singapore.
9 He is staying in Australia for more than a week.
10 Peter is leaving Australia on 4th February.

Writing

F WRITING ACTIVITY

DESCRIBING PEOPLE

Listen again to Peter Parker talking about his trip to Australia. The write a short newspaper article about it.
You will need about 150 words. Begin like this:

Peter Parker, who recently won an essay competition on the subject of 'The journey of a lifetime', is starting off on his own journey of a lifetime next week.

Test 1

1 WRITE OUT THE FOLLOWING SENTENCES, PUTTING THE VERB IN THE CORRECT TENSE.

▷ *Example: I/your sister/in the town/this morning (see)*
I saw your sister in the town this morning.

1 I/never/chocolate cake (eat)
2 My brother/usually/to work (walk)
3 Last week/Tom/a new car (buy)
4 I can see the postman. He/outside our house (stand)
5 We are off to Spain next week. We/by air (go)
6 I'm sorry, I/some milk/while you were out (spill)
7 They always/the 6 o'clock news/on the radio (listen to)
8 You can't have my pen just now. I/a letter (write)
9 I'm afraid we/all the apples/last night (eat)
10 She/that picture/when we were at the seaside (draw)

20 Marks

2 RE-WRITE THE FOLLOWING SENTENCES, PUTTING THE VERBS IN THE SIMPLE PAST AND ADDING A DIFFERENT POINT IN TIME *(eg. last year)* IN EACH CASE.

▷ *Example: He finishes the job.*
He **finished** *the job* **last week**.

1 We argue a lot about it.
2 He dies.
3 They throw the fish back.
4 I take the old car back.
5 She wears jeans.
6 Concorde flies over.
7 It bites the postman.
8 They show him the garden.
9 I think about her.
10 She comes to see me.

20 Marks

UNIT
5

3 USE A FORM OF THE WORD IN BRACKETS TO COMPLETE SENTENCES:

▷ Example: The ice made the road _____. (slip)
  The ice made the road **slippery.**

1 Peter has a very _____ job (bore)
2 This is a very _____ necklace. (value)
3 We're _____ at a seaside hotel. (stay)
4 The boys went fishing and they _____ three fish. (catch)
5 The policmen were after him, so he _____ in the wood. (hide)
6 He tried to sell the _____ silver. (steal)
7 Caruso was a very _____ singer. (fame)
8 John's brother is a very _____ young man. (ambition)
9 She's five years old and has an _____ friend. (imagine)
10 I think J.D. Salinger writes very _____ . (good)

20 Marks

4 COMPLETE THE FOLLOWING SENTENCES WITH: _SOMEBODY_, _SOMETHING_, _ANYBODY_ OR _ANYTHING_.

▷ Example: Does — know Mr Parker?
  Does **anybody** know Mr Parker?

1 We didn't buy _____ at the supermarket.
2 There must be _____ we can do.
3 Look out! I think _____ is coming.
4 There isn't _____ in the basket.
5 He told me _____ very interesting.
6 I haven't got _____ more to say.

Complete the following sentences with **much** or **many.**

7 How _____ cakes did you buy?
8 Do _____ people live there?
9 We haven't _____ time, I'm afraid.
10 How _____ fruit did you eat?

10 Marks

5 BELOW IS THE TEXT OF A LETTER FROM JENNIE TO MOLLY. WRITE IT OUT IN THE FORM OF A LETTER, USING TWO PARAGRAPHS AND PUTTING IN CAPITAL LETTERS AND PUNCTUATION, WHERE NECESSARY.

college road sheffield 8th august dear molly thank you very much for your letter i'm so glad to hear that you are pleased with your new home it sounds very nice unfortunately i can't accept your invitation to come and see you next weekend my sister and i are going to spain on saturday for a short holiday love to you both jennie

30 Marks

Total Marks: 100

35

UNIT

5

A WHY WERE SILENT MOVIES SO POPULAR?

It is not surprising that the old silent films were immensely popular. They were made by professionals who understood exactly what their audiences wanted. The hero was brave, handsome and strong, the heroine charming and beautiful. The villain, on the other hand, was unspeakably wicked.

At the beginning of the film we meet the hero. Through no fault of his own he is down on his luck. He has no money and no job. If, by any chance, he does have a job, then he works for a brutal and unsympathetic employer and is about to get the sack. The heroine, too, is poor but honest. She lost both her parents in a tragic accident. She is alone in the world and the villain wants to marry her. He is, of course, old enough to be her father. She, however, dreams of romance.

She sees the hero and he sees her. They look into one another's eyes. Their hands touch. Their hearts beat faster. But fate soon tears them apart. They suffer terribly. Then, just when everything seems quite hopeless, fate brings them together again. The hero inherits a fortune. The villain receives his well deserved punishment and our happy young lovers walk off hand in hand into the setting sun . . . .

QUESTIONS ON THE TEXT

1 Can you name any of the actors who became famous acting in silent films?

2 Can you name any popular actors and actresses of today?

3 Who was brave? Can you think of another word that means the same as brave?

4 Is **handsome** the same as **pretty**? If you think they are different, think of some occasions when we might use **handsome** and where **pretty** would be a better word.

5 Someone who is **down on his luck** has been unlucky. Think of some things that might happen to somebody and so cause us to say: 'He was very unlucky'.

6 A friend of yours is in trouble. Usually, in a situation like this, you would feel very sorry for your friend, but in this case you feel quite unsympathetic. What happened?

7 Can you think of any tragic accidents reported in the newspapers recently?

8 **Romance** is a noun. Find out what the adjective is. Think of some nouns you could use **roman** . . . with.

9 What is the opposite of hopeless? Think of a situation that seemed hopeless and then of something that happened that made it seem more . . . (the opposite of hopeless).

10 The hero described in the text was fortunate in at least two ways. What were they?

Exercise

B WORD BUILDING

Write out this short extract from an autobiography, putting in the missing words and phrases from the list below:

beam – circle – curtain – projector – row – screen – staircase – swing doors – tickets – torch

The foyer of the cinema seemed very grand. My father bought our ____1____ and we went up a wide ____2____ and through a pair of ____3____, behind which was a thick, red ____4____. Inside the cinema it was quite dark, except for the powerful ____5____ of light thrown onto the ____6____ by the ____7____. The usherette shone her ____8____ in our direction and indicated two empty seats. But my father whispered something to her and she led us down to the very front ____9____ of the ____10____. I was thrilled.

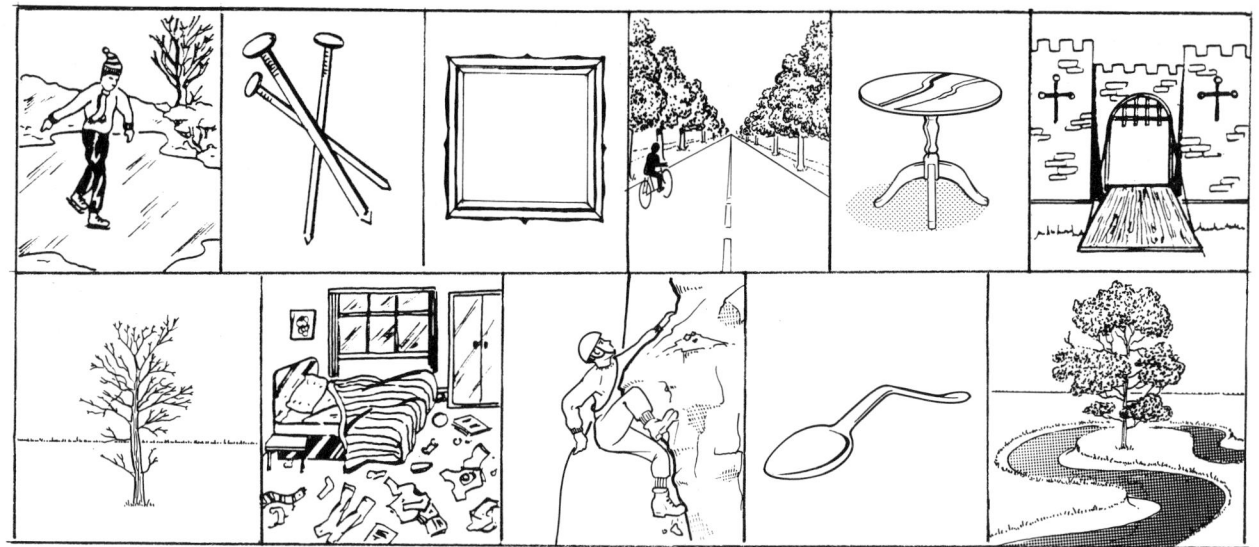

Exercise

C TALKING ABOUT THE PHYSICAL APPEARANCE OF THINGS. MATCH UP THE ADJECTIVES WITH THE OBJECTS. USE EACH ADJECTIVE ONCE ONLY.

ancient – bare – bent – dangerous – pointed – shiny – slippery – square – untidy – wide – winding

Exercise

D TALKING ABOUT PEOPLE'S CHARACTERS. MATCH THE PEOPLE WITH THE ADJECTIVES. (YOU WILL FINISH UP WITH THREE SPARE ADJECTIVES).

aggressive – brave – dishonest – energetic – generous – honest – kind – lazy – lonely – mean – rude – selfish – sensitive – sensible – stubborn

1 Tom is always thinking about himself.
2 Peter shows a lot of courage.
3 Mary has a lot of energy.
4 Ruth doesn't like working at all.
5 You can trust Susan completely.
6 John hates spending money.
7 Anne is always giving things away.
8 It's very easy to hurt Philip's feelings.
9 Frank has no friends. This makes him sad.
10 You can be sure that Andrew won't do silly things.
11 When Joan gets an idea into her head, its impossible to change her mind.
12 Simon doesn't always tell the truth and you can't trust him with money.

Write down the three extra adjectives. They refer to Richard, Laura and David.
Write a sentence about each like the ones above. Use a dictionary if necessary.

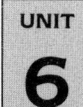

UNIT
6

38

E TALKING ABOUT EXPERIENCES. HERE ARE SOME ADJECTIVES WE USE TO DESCRIBE EXPERIENCES:

amusing – boring – exciting – frightening – interesting – uncomfortable – unusual – tragic

Think of an experience to go with each adjective.

▷ *Example: boring*
> *You don't like tennis. Then you could say:*
> *'We went to watch the tennis. It was very boring'.*
> *or*
> *'There was a programme on TV about the dangers of smoking. I found it boring'.*

SPECIAL POINTS TO NOTE

We use adjectives to describe people or things. Sometimes we put the adjectives in front of the noun:

an **unsympathetic** employer
silent films
a **handsome** stranger
a **tragic** accident

Sometimes we put the adjective after the noun/and verb:

The hero was **brave**.
The films were **popular**.
The heroine was **poor**.
The situation seems **hopeless**.
The villain looked angry.
This pudding tastes **delicious**.

Note that there are a small number of adjectives that end in -ly. Since many adverbs also end in -ly (See unit 7) it is important that students remember that these are adjectives. Below is a list of the most important.

NB
ADJECTIVES!!

early:	He took an **early** train.
friendly:	Her new colleagues were very **friendly.**
unfriendly:	The children were rather **unfriendly.**
likely:	He is the **likely** winner of the competition.
unlikely:	It was an **unlikely** place to find him.
lonely:	As he had no brothers or sisters he was a **lonely** child.
lovely:	It was a **lovely** wedding.

Listening

F LISTENING

RADIO ADS

You are going to hear four radio advertisements.

Before you listen to the tape, study the following vocabulary:

craftsman:	highly trained worker
leather:	animal skin treated and used to make things
catalogue:	list of goods, often with illustrations
stationery:	writing paper, envelopes, pens, pencils etc.
sample:	example of something for sale
battery:	device which produces electricity
guarantee:	formal promise that an article is of good quality
patio:	area outside the house with a stone floor, used in fine weather
frame:	support around which something is stretched

Listen to four advertisements and decide in each case what product is being advertised.

Then listen again to each advertisement, several times if necessary, and write down any of the adjectives or other interesting expressions used to make the product seem attractive.

Writing

G WRITING ACTIVITY

DESCRIBING PEOPLE

People can be:	tall, short, dark, fair, black, pale, fat, slim, thin, elderly, middle-aged, or young.
Men can be:	broad-shouldered, they can have a beard, a moustache, tattoos, thinning hair, or be bald, or handsome.

Choose any two of the following people.
Give them names and write short descriptions of them.
You will need about 50 words for each description.

41

MAN ATTACKS PAINTING

A man armed with a knife caused considerable damage to a valuable painting in the art gallery yesterday. The incident took place at approximately 4 o'clock in the afternoon in room number 10. The attendants on duty at that time were Arthur Woods and Nigel Perkins. Apart from the attendants the gallery was almost deserted.

Woods and Perkins say they had no warning of anything unusual until a middle-aged man wearing a dark blue overcoat and a blue beret suddenly produced a sharp knife and began slashing viciously at a fifteenth century religious painting. Woods immediately shouted a warning, whereupon the man cried out in a foreign language, dropped the knife and rushed past him into the street.

However two members of the public say they noticed a man wearing a blue overcoat behaving strangely in room number 10 a short while before the attack took place. The man was blinking nervously and at the same time muttering to himself quite loudly in a language they could not understand.

Asked about the condition of the painting after the attack, the curator, Mr Tony Robinson said: 'Fortunately the knife used in the attack was so sharp that the cuts in the canvas are fairly neat and tidy. The actual paint wasn't seriously damaged. As a result it should be possible to repair the painting satisfactorily'. The motive for the attack is still unknown.

Reading

A WHERE DID THIS ATTACK HAPPEN AND WHY?

QUESTIONS ON THE TEXT

1 The man was armed with a knife. What else might someone be armed with?
2 What time did the incident take place?
3 Were there many visitors in the gallery at the time the man was there?
4 Describe the way in which the man attacked the painting.
5 What was it that made Woods almost sure that the man was not English?
6 Why did the two people in the gallery notice the man?
7 Explain why the cuts in the canvas were so neat and tidy.
8 How badly was the actual paint damaged?

Exercise

B WORD BUILDING

Study these 10 words and phrases, which are all connected with art or the theatre. Then match them with the definitions below:

canvas – landscape – oil painting – portrait – print – sculptor – scenery – stage – statue – sculpture

1 artist who makes figures of people, animals, etc.
2 material often used for painting on
3 large figure of a person or animal made of stone, metal, etc.
4 painting of a person
5 platform in a theatre where the actors perform
6 painting of a view of the countryside
7 painted background in a theatre
8 copy of a painting made using a machine
9 picture painted using oil paints
10 art of making figures out of stone, wood, metal, etc.

Exercise

C MOST OF THE RULES CONCERNING THE POSITION OF ADVERBS IN A SENTENCE ARE COMPLICATED AND NOT VERY HELPFUL. BUT REMEMBER ONE RULE. NEVER PUT AN ADVERB BETWEEN A VERB AND ITS DIRECT OBJECT.

▷ *Examples:* **Sadly** *Martha packed her suitcase.*
Martha **sadly** *packed her suitacase.*
Martha packed her suitcase **sadly**.

All the above sentences are possible, but <u>sadly</u> could never be placed between <u>packed</u> (the verb) and <u>her suitcase</u> (the object)

Here are some useful adverbs. Work in pairs and check their meanings. You may need a dictionary.

angrily – carefully – cheerfully – loudly – nervously – quickly – sensibly – slowly – terribly – rudely

Below are some sentences. Re-write them, adding one suitable adverb chosen from the list above, to each.

1 Tom went to see the doctor about the pain in his chest.
2 The train moved out of the station.
3 Harriet changed her mind about the dress.
4 Peter's foot hurt.
5 Richard put the phone down.
6 Agnes replaced the vase on the shelf.
7 A man pushed in front of Doris.
8 Mr Wagstaffe whistled to himself as he washed the dishes.
9 Max's footsteps echoed on the wooden staircase.
10 Arthur waited for his interviews.

When you have finished, compare your sentences with those of other students and discuss your answers with your teacher.

As you continue your studies, become a collector of interesting sentences containing adverbs. In this way you will develop your feeling for the language and eventually you will **know** where to put your adverbs.

D HERE ARE SOME SENTENCES CONTAINING OTHER USEFUL ADVERBS. VERY FEW OF THEM END IN -LY AND EACH OF THEM IS WORTH STUDYING CAREFULLY:

Concorde flies very **high**. (high in the air)
Dexter obtained the information from a **highly** placed official. (The official held a high position)
Some missiles travel very **low**. (near the ground)
The invitation arrived **late**. (not early enough)
There have been a lot of accidents on this bit of road **lately** (recently)
These modern trains go very **fast**. (quickly)
The boys are working very **hard**. (with a lot of effort)
Poor Roger and Daphne have **hardly** any money. (very little money)
Sally's quite **tired** after her journey. (very tired)
The tomb was **quite** empty. (completely empty)
It wasn't sunny but it was **fairly** warm. (warm in a positive sense – not cold)
You look **rather** warm, Harry. (too warm to feel comfortable)

Below are 12 questions. Work in pairs and answer the questions taking your information from the sentences above. These are in no particular order.

1 Why is it difficult to detect them on the radar screen?
2 Why do modern jet aircraft need pressurised cabins?
3 How is it that we can travel there so quickly?
4 Why is the information probably correct?
5 Why didn't she go to the party?

6 What did they find in the tomb?

7 You think Harry probably ran all the way. Explain why.

8 Why can't they buy a new car?

9 Does Sally want to go out this evening?

10 Why weren't they disappointed that it wasn't sunny?

11 Why should we drive carefully?

12 Why do they deserve a short holiday?

SPECIAL POINTS TO NOTE

There are different kinds of adverb. Adverbs that tell us how often things happen – <u>usually</u>, <u>sometimes</u>, <u>never</u> – are frequently used together with the Simple Present tense.

▷ *Example: She never travels by bus.*

Adverbs like: <u>now</u>, <u>soon</u>, <u>yesterday</u> are called Adverbs of Time.

▷ *Examples: Relax, the train is coming **soon**.*
*I saw her **yesterday**.*

We use some adverbs to describe how people do things. Such adverbs are often formed by adding -ly to the adjective.

▷ *Examples: The man started slashing **viciously** at a painting.*
*He was behaving **strangely**.*
*He was blinking **nervously**.*

We also use adverbs to modify adjectives and other adverbs:

▷ *Examples: He used a **very** sharp knife.*
*The cuts are **fairly** neat.*
*He was muttering **quite** loudly to himself.*
*The man produced the knife **too** quickly for the attendant to stop him.*

Note the forms of the following adverbs which do not end in -<u>ly</u>:

Adjective	Adverb
good	well
fast	fast
high	high
low	low

Note also useful ways of expressing adverbial ideas with these words where the adjective ends in -<u>ly</u>.

Adjective	Adverb	
friendly	in a friendly way	(She smiles in a friendly way)
likely	probably	(He is probably coming to the party)
lovely	beautifully	(He cut her hair beautifully)

E LISTENING

AN INTERVIEW

MAKING A GOOD IMPRESSION

You are going to hear a discussion about interviews.

Before you listen to the tape study the following vocabulary:

interview: dialogue aimed at finding out information
mention: speak or write about
appointment: meeting
hot and bothered: in a nervous state
compose yourself: calm yourself
presumably: one imagines that
qualifications: talents that make one fit to do a job
ordeal: hard, painful experience
neat: tidy
apply for: ask for (usually in writing)
generation gap: different ideas held by younger and older people
advertising agency: organisation responsible for creating advertisements
applicant: person applying for a job

Listen to Judy Christie discussing with Mark Taylor the best way to approach an interview. Mark gives a number of tips to young people going for an interview. Listen to the dialogue, several times if necessary, and make a list of them.

Discussion:
What do you think of Mark's advice?
Can you think of any more tips for young people going to an interview?
Do you believe it is really possible to enjoy an interview?
What about the interviewer(s)? How do you think they feel about interviews.

F WRITING ACTIVITY

USING ADVERBS

Read the description of a young man going for an interview. Then re-write the description adding some or all of the following adverbs:

already — early — exactly — in a friendly way — nervously — quite — rather — slowly — still — too

Richard caught a train to the city. As he didn't have to be there till 10 o'clock, he walked from the station to Smith Street. He got there. He went in through the big, glass doors. A pretty girl behind the reception desk asked if she could help him. He explained that he was there for an interview. She smiled and pointed to a row of chairs on the other side of the reception area. A girl and two other young men were there. They glanced at him but didn't speak. He knew what was in their minds. How many more applicants would turn up for this one job?

UNIT

7

A WHAT IS THE CUTTY SARK? WHERE IS IT NOW?

Just over 100 years ago steamships began to replace the beautiful old clipper ships. Gradually the clippers disappeared, until now only the Cutty Sark remains.

It was built in Scotland and launched in 1869. At that time tea was a particularly valuable cargo and there was a special prize for the sailing ship making the fastest time from China to Britain. The Cutty Sark made eight of these voyages, carrying over a million pounds of tea on each occasion.

Later it sailed regularly between Australia and Britain with cargoes of wool, and it was during this period that a young apprentice called William Dowman saw it sail by. It was a sight he never forgot.

Eventually, as the old clippers became uneconomic, the Cutty Sark was sold to a Portuguese owner. It sailed under the Portuguese flag for nearly thirty years, often loaded with cargoes of coal.

Then the young apprentice, now an experienced sea captain, suddenly discovered that it was for sale and he purchased it and brought it back to Britain. Captain Dowman restored it to its former glory and for a number of years it was used as a training ship.

Finally, about 40 years ago, the Cutty Sark was towed up the river Thames to the dry dock specially built for it at Greenwich. There some 350,000 people from all over the world visit it every year.

COMPREHENSION QUESTIONS

1 What caused the decline in the importance of the old clippers?

2 How long ago did this happen?

3 When was the Cutty Sark launched?

4 Give the names of three different cargoes it carried.

5 What was it that William Dowman never forgot?

6 Why did the Cutty Sark sail under the Portuguese flag?

7 Captain Dowman spent a lot of money on the Cutty Sark. Explain how.

8 When was the Cutty Sark moved to its dock at Greenwich?

B WORD BUILDING

The words below are all the names of different kinds
of boat or ship.
Match them with the definitions below:

aircraft carrier – canoe – cruise liner – lifeboat – motor
boat – rowing boat – submarine – tanker – tug – yacht

1 boat that uses wind power
2 big ship that carries oil
3 little ship with a powerful motor that pulls big ships
4 warship that can go under the sea
5 warship that carries aeroplanes
6 big ship that takes passengers for pleasant
voyages
7 boat used to rescue sailors in danger
8 small craft propelled by a man using oars
9 small craft propelled by a man using paddles
10 small craft with an engine at the back that can go
very fast

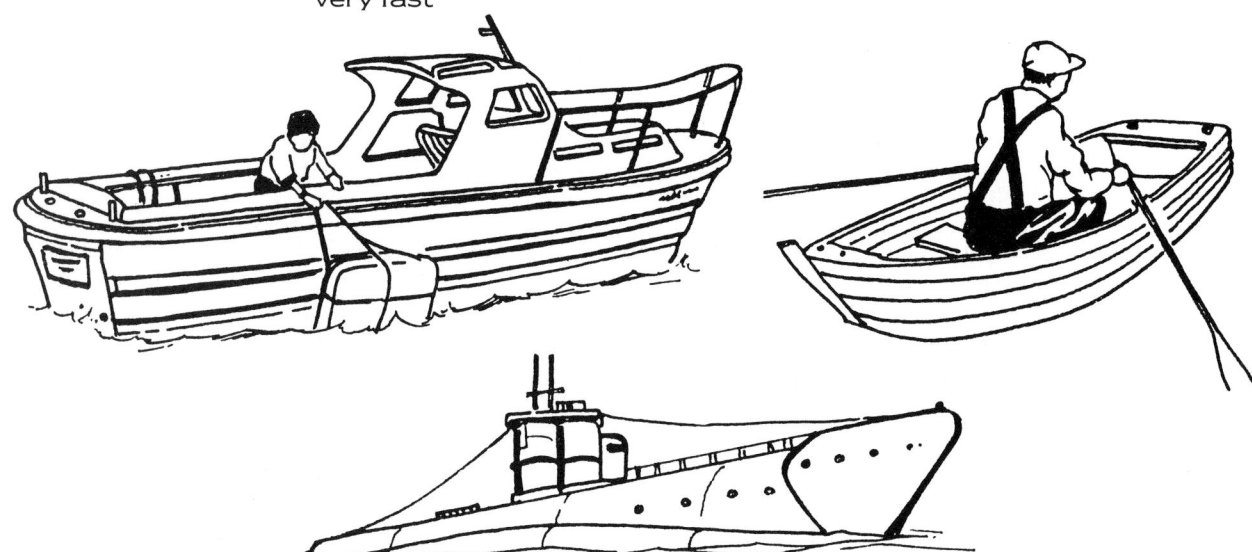

C WORK IN PAIRS. MATCH UP THE HISTORICAL FACTS WITH EXPRESSIONS WITH <u>AGO</u>:

1 The first men walked on the moon – 1969
2 The French revolution took place – 1784
3 Hitler came to power – 1933
4 The Suez Canal was opened – 1869
5 Alexander the Great lived – 356 BC
6 The Russian revolution occurred – 1917
7 The Romans invaded Britain – 43 AD
8 The Great Fire of London took place – 1666
9 The Russians put the first satellite into space –
1957
10 The first postage stamps appeared – 1840

a	about	2,350 years ago
b	'	1,950 years ago
c	'	325 years ago
d	'	200 years ago
e	'	150 years ago
f	'	120 years ago
g	'	75 years ago
h	'	60 years ago
i	'	30 years ago
j	'	20 years ago

D JUDY WRIGHT IS A JOURNALIST. LOOK AT HER DIARY FOR THE MONTH OF JUNE AND SAY HOW LONG AGO SHE FILLED THE ENGAGEMENTS MARKED.

Use phrases like: a week ago, a short while ago, a few days ago, two days ago, a couple of weeks ago
Today is the 21st June.

JUNE

1 Travel to New York—interview with editor of Vogue.	16 Return to London.
2	17
3	18 Attend film premiere of Money, Money, Money.
4	19 Lunch with editor of Woman.
5 Interview with Gloria Kane (film actress).	20
6	21
7	22
8 Travel to Washington—interview with Martha Harris.	23
9	24
10	25
11	26
12 Attend first night of new play Maggie.	27
13	28
14	29
15 Fly to Paris— attend fashion show.	30

Now work in pairs. Think of three or four further entries for the diary and say how long ago Judy filled these engagements.

E WORK IN PAIRS. THINK OF SOME INTERESTING THINGS THAT HAVE HAPPENED TO YOU. HOW LONG AGO DID THEY HAPPEN?

SPECIAL POINTS TO NOTE

We use <u>ago</u> with a time expression and the Simple Past tense to say when something happened.

Examples: *The Cutty Sark made its last voyage* **over 30 years ago.**
How long ago *did it happen?*
It all happened **a long time ago.**

F LISTENING

OLD FRIENDS

Manfred, Lisa and Thierry were all together five years ago. They met again recently in Paris. Listen to their conversation, then do the exercises below:

Answer the following questions.

1 Why were Manfred, Lisa and Thierry in London?
2 What nationality do you think Manfred is?
3 What organisation does Lisa work for?
4 Explain why she often comes into contact with travellers.
5 What product does Manfred's firm deal in?
6 Why did Thierry leave the hotel business?
7 What businesss is he in now?
8 What happened to Marina?
9 Where does Yvette work?
10 Where does Milo come from?

Listen to the tape again and make a note of how long ago the following things happened:

11 Lisa joined Swiss Railways.
12 Manfred first worked for his present employer.
13 Thierry gave up his job in the hotel.
14 Marina got married.
15 Thierry had a postcard from Yvette.
16 Manfred last wrote to Milo.

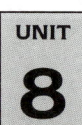

UNIT

8

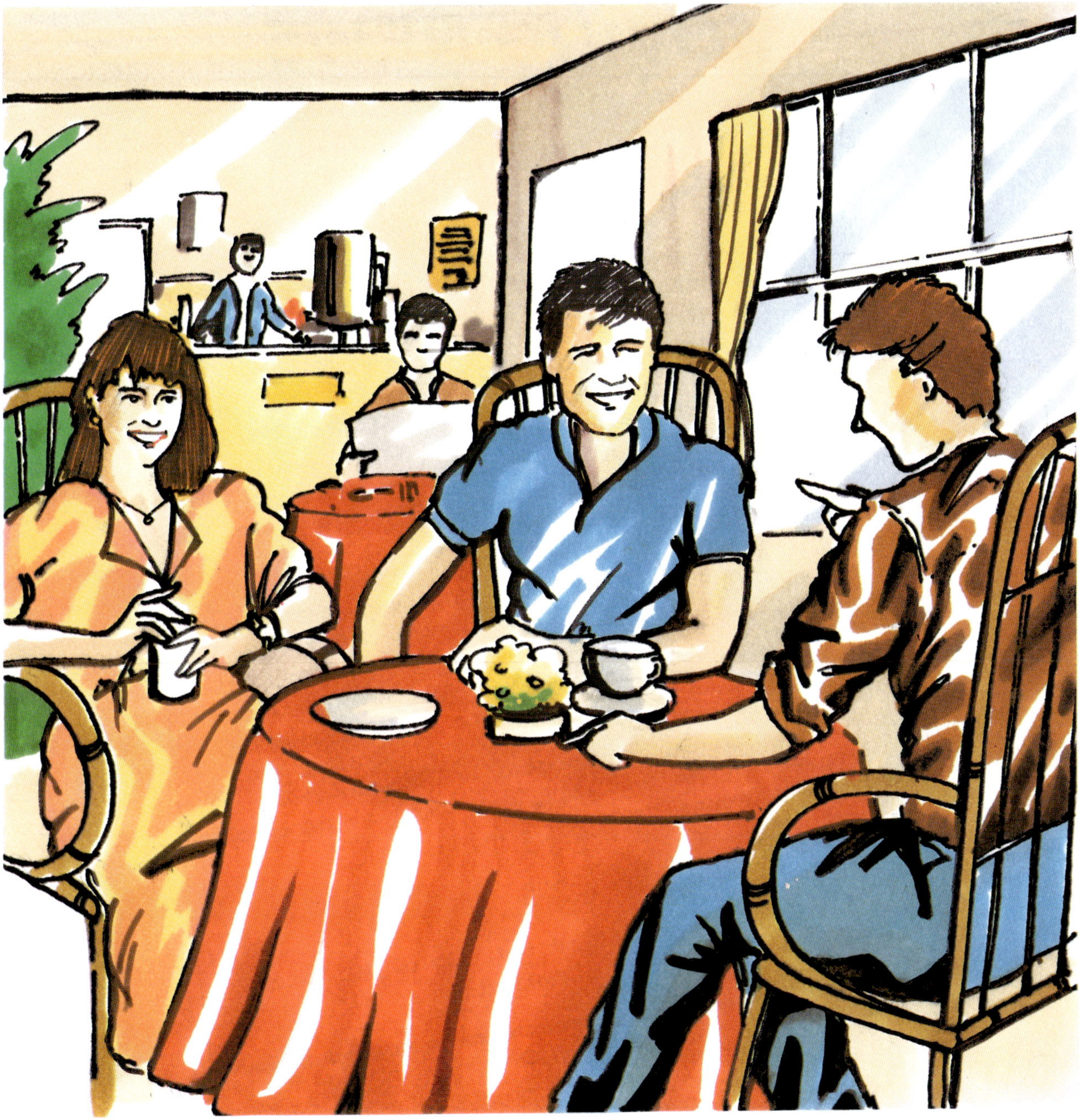

Writing

G WRITING ACTIVITY

USING THE PAST TENSE

Write eight sentences about your life using expressions with **ago.**

▷ *Examples: I left school two years ago.*
A few years ago we spent a wonderful holiday on the island of Kos.

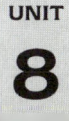

12, Abingdon Street
London SW16
7th June

Dear Emma,

Thanks for your letter. I was glad to hear that your Mum was getting better.

I have news. Guess what? I found a flat at last. It's really two rooms and a toilet above a grocer's shop and I don't quite know how to put this but it smells a bit at the moment. Never mind. We're going to redecorate the place completely and the landlord's going to put in a new handbasin. It's in a marvellous position, though, in a small street off Kensington High Road, really close to central London.

I can't afford the rent by myself, but Ralph is going to share it with me. After a lot of negotiating, we've agreed that I'm going to pay £3 a week. more than him, but I'm going to have the bedroom. We're going to buy a sofa bed for the sitting room and Ralph's going to sleep on that.

I'm going to buy an electric kettle so that we can make our own tea and coffee, but we're not going to become terribly domesticated and do our own cooking. No time for that really and there are plenty of cheap cafés around here.

Love to all the family,
Gary.

P.S. That's my new address at the top of the letter. We're going to move in on Saturday.

COMPREHENSION QUESTIONS

1 Who was ill?
2 Describe the flat.
3 What's so good about the location?
4 Why is Ralph going to come and live with him?
5 Where's Ralph going to sleep?
6 Are Ralph and Gary going to take it in turns to do the cooking?
7 Why/why not?
8 Where are they going to eat?

B WORD BUILDING

Emma's mother has had a problem with her health. Match up things that might be wrong with someone with **the symptoms** and possible **forms of treatment**.

Problem:
1. Headache
2. Mumps
3. Sprained ankle
4. Whooping cough
5. Measles

Symptoms:
a. High temperature. Runny nose. Pink spots on neck, forehead and face.
b. Pain when swallowing. Swelling below ears on neck and face.
c. Starts as an ordinary cold. Dry repeated cough. Vomiting.
d. Pain in head, particularly when moving about.
e. Swelling and pain in joints.

Treatment:
v. Go to bed. Drink a lot of liquid. Shield eyes from lights.
w. Rest in bed. Take paracetamol.
x. Call doctor. Doctor may prescribe antibiotics or cough medicines.
y. Take aspirins or paracetamol. Rest in bed. Drink rose hip syrup, but avoid orange or lemon juice.
z. Bathe alternatively in hot and cold water. Rest as much as possible.

Exercise ▷

C PRACTISE USING <u>GOING TO</u> TO ANNOUNCE YOUR DECISION.

Example: You could travel by train or you could hire a car.
*Student: I'm not **going to** travel by train. I'm **going to** hire a car.*
or
*I'm **not going to** hire a car. I'm **going to** travel by train.*

1. You could have tea or you could have coffee.
2. You could go to the zoo today or you could go tomorrow.
3. You could buy the cassette or you could buy the record.
4. You could go to the cinema or you could watch television.
5. You could telephone your brother or you could write him a letter.
6. You could borrow some money or you could wait until pay day.
7. You could give your aunt a box of chocolates for her birthday or you could give her a plant.
8. You could go to the theatre on your own or you could ask Jim to come with you.
9. You could telephone tonight or you could wait until morning.
10. You could go for a drive or you could stay at home.

UNIT
9

D LOOK AT THIS SENTENCE:

They sold their house, but they're **going to** buy another one.

Complete the following sentences in a similar way, using **going to**.

1 We didn't have a holiday last year, but . . .
2 John cooked the dinner yesterday, but . . .
3 I'm afraid we lost two of your tennis balls, but . . .
4 I walked to work yesterday, but . . .
5 Someone stole their car, but . . .
6 She didn't vote in the last election, but . . .
7 He travelled to Europe from Montevideo on a very old cargo ship, but . . .
8 I wrote to them and they never answered, but . . .
9 He forgot to bring his camera today, but . . .
10 His father refused to lend him the money, but . . .

E BELOW YOU WILL FIND DESCRIPTIONS OF SOME DRAMATIC EVENTS THAT MIGHT OCCUR IN A FILM.

Example: A very heavily loaded aeroplane is attempting to take off from a short landing strip in the jungle.
An onlooker says: **'He's going to hit the trees'.**

Make further predictions:

1 A racing driver who takes a lot of risks crashes. The car is wrecked, but the driver is OK this time.
Another driver says: (kill)

2 The building is on fire. The firemen are searching for people overcome by smoke. The roof is in a dangerous state. Something falls.
A fireman shouts: (fall in)

3 A small boat has overturned in the swiftly flowing river. A child is thrown into the water.
An onlooker cries out: (drown)

4 A small plane has crashed. It's on fire. Desperately two men struggle to free the pilot. The flames are creeping closer to the petrol tank.
One man says: (blow up)

5 A man is swimming frantically across a jungle river. The crocodile is getting closer and closer.
An onlooker says: (get)

6 The fighter plane is badly damaged. The pilot jumps out, but his parachute hasn't opened.
A man on the ground cries: (not open)

UNIT
9

NOTE HOW WE FORM

Statements:

I'm You're He's/She's We're You're They're	going to	light a fire.

Negatives:

I'm You're He's/She's We're You're They're	not going to	start a forest fire.

Questions:

Am I Are you Is he/Is she Are we Are you Are they	going to	cook a meal?

SPECIAL POINTS TO NOTE

The _**Going to**_ future is very useful. We use it

a   To tell people about things we **intend** to do or to announce decisions that we or other people have made.

▷   _Examples: My camera's not working very well._ **I'm going to** _buy a new one._
**John's going to** take that summer job at the restaurant.
**I'm not going to** go to the disco. I'm too tired.

b   For making predictions, particularly when the speaker is behaving in an emotional way.

▷   _Examples: Look out._ **We're going to** _crash._
Careful. **You're going to** _knock over that vase._

F LISTENING

CAREER CHOICES

You are going to hear four young people Debbie, John, Frieda and Tony, talking about their hopes for the future.

Listening

UNIT

9

Before you listen to the tape, study the following vocabulary:

retail:	sales (to the public)
branch:	field
physics:	sciences dealing wih matter and energy
staff:	people who work there
assuming:	presuming

Listen to the tape, more than once if necessary, and answer the following questions:

1 Where's Debbie going to study?
2 What's she going to study?
3 Why?
4 What's John going to be?
5 What's he going to do when he leaves school?
6 What's he particularly interested in?
7 Where's Frieda going to study?
8 What's she going to be?
9 What does she say, that she thinks may surprise people?
10 Why does Tony feel ashamed?
11 When is he going to decide on a career?
12 What does he intend to do before he settles down?

Writing

G   WRITING ACTIVITY

USING THE FUTURE

Think of yourself at the age of 16. Imagine you are invited to appear on the same programme as Debbie, Frieda, John and Tony.

Remember the question. What do you hope to do when you leave school?
Write the answer you might give, in 50 to 80 words.

PASSPORT PANIC

A WHAT EXACTLY IS MR HARRISON'S PROBLEM?

The telephone rang in the British Embassy abroad. A young woman answered. 'British Embassy. Can I help you?'

'My name is Harrison', said the voice at the other end of the line, 'Percy Harrison. I **am** a British subject . . . and I have a problem'.

'Do you want to discuss it over the telephone, Mr Harrison, or would you prefer to come round to the Embassy?'

'Well, I'm not sure what to do. I can't find my passport'.

'Do you mean you've lost it?' enquired the woman.

'Oh I don't think I've **lost** it', replied Harrison, 'I just can't find it'.

'When did you last have it?'

'At the airport. I know I had it at the airport when I arrived. The immigration official looked at it. I think he put a stamp in it'.

'And you haven't seen it since? Perhaps you forgot to pick it up when you left the immigration desk. Have you rung the airport?'

'No. I'm sure I had it when I got to the hotel', said Harrison slowly.

'Do you think that someone has stolen it?'

'I suppose it's possible'. Harrison hesitated ' . . . er . . . What if I can't find it? Can you provide me with a document of some sort?'

'Yes, we can arrange that', replied the woman crisply, 'providing of course that you come round to the Embassy and give us some further information'.

'Thank you. Thank you very much'. Harrison put the phone down.

Ten minutes later the telephone in the Embassy rang again. This time a man wearing a smart blue suit answered the phone. 'British Embassy'.

'It's all right. I've found it,' shouted Harrison.

The man in the Embassy moved the receiver further away from his ear.

'I'm afraid I don't quite understand', he murmured.

'My passport . . . I've found it. It was in the pocket of my white jacket'.

'Ah well. That's all right then'.

'I thought I'd let you know'.

'Quite'. The man at the Embassy replaced the receiver thoughtfully. 'Too much sun, perhaps', he muttered to himself.

59

UNIT
10

COMPREHENSION QUESTIONS

1 Explain why Mr Harrison says, 'I **am** a British subject'.
2 Why is Mr Harrison so sure that he had his passport at the airport?
3 When does Mr Harrison next remember having his passport?
4 What must Mr Harrison do if he can't find his passport?
5 Why does Mr Harrison ring the Embassy a second time?
6 Why is the man at the Embassy a little confused by Mr Harrison's call
7 Ask where Mr Harrison found the passport.
8 What does the man at the Embassy mean by the words 'too much sun perhaps'?

B WORD BUILDING

Exercise

Mr Harrison **lost** his passport. The opposite of <u>lose</u> is **find. All the verbs below have been used in previous units. Work with a partner to find their opposites. Use your dictionary if necessary.**

1 buy	sell
2 go to sleep	
3 open	
4 appear	
5 attack	
6 damage	
7 criticise	
8 stop	
9 receive	
10 lend	

C HERE IS SOME INFORMATION ABOUT MR HARRISON:

Exercise

He is 50 years old and he lived with his parents until they both died recently.
For the past 20 years he has worked in a Government office. He has just sold the family home in London and bought a small house at the seaside. He has retired on a small pension. This is the first time he has been abroad for a holiday.

Now ask and answer the following questions:

1 Ask what has happened to Mr Harrison's parents.
2 Answer the question.
3 Ask if he still works in the same office.

UNIT
10

4 Answer the question and explain why.
5 Ask if he still lives in the family home.
6 Answer the question and say what he has done.
7 Ask if Mr Harrison has often been abroad for holidays.
8 Answer the question.

D LOOK AT THIS EXAMPLE. THEN SAY WHAT'S HAPPENED IN EACH CASE IN THE FOLLOWING SITUATIONS.

▷ *Example: Peter's car won't move. The petrol gauge indicates zero.*
Peter isn't pleased.
He's run out of petrol.

1 George is getting his breakfast. The doorbell rang and he went to answer it. Now the toast in the toaster is black and there's a smell of burning.

2 Cecile is washing the dishes. The water's very hot. Suddenly she finds that she has a cup in one hand and its handle in the other.

3 It's windy tonight. A window was open and Tom got up to close it unfortunately he made a lot of noise and now the baby's crying.

4 After the party, Joe took Lucille home. He said goodnight to her outside her front door. Now Lucille is on her hands and knees searching for something.

5 Mr Gladwin wants to watch the 6 o'clock news on the television. His watch indicates that it's just 6 o'clock, but it's 20 minutes slow.

6 Mr and Mrs Barber and their baby daughter are sitting on a sandy beach. The baby is playing with the sand. Suddenly her dad notices that she has a diamond ring in her hand.

7 Ron and Harry are camping. They lit a fire, but the wood was damp. The flames got smaller and smaller and now there are no flames.

8 Mr and Mrs Sutcliffe enjoyed the film on the television. Now Mr Sutcliffe has turned off the set and they are going to bed.

E LOOK AT THIS DIALOGUE

Have you visited Hong Kong?
Yes, I have.
When did you go there?
I went there last year.

Note that as soon as a time expression is introduced, the speaker changes from the Present Perfect to the Simple Past tense. If the answer is *No, I haven't* the conversation comes to an end.

UNIT
10

Work in pairs. Ask and answer questions. Practise changing to the Simple Past when the time expression is introduced. Allow the conversation to continue briefly, where possible.

1 Ask your partner if he/she has seen (any new films).
2 Ask your partner if he/she has ever flown in an aeroplane.
3 Ask your partner if he/she has ever visited the United States (or any country)
4 Ask your partner if he/she has ever bought something and later regretted it.
5 Ask your partner if he/she has ever fallen off a horse, bicycle or scooter.
6 Ask your partner if he/she has ever found anything valuable.
7 Ask your partner if he/she has ever been to hospital for an operation.
8 Ask your partner if he/she has ever broken anything belonging to somebody else.
9 Ask your partner if he/she has ever lent something to somebody and not got it back.
10 Ask your partner if he/she has heard (any new record).

NOTE HOW WE FORM THE PRESENT PERFECT

Statements:

I've (I have) You've	
He's, she's (He has, she has)	lost it.
We've etc.	

Negatives:

I haven't You haven't	
He hasn't, she hasn't	found it.
We haven't etc.	

Questions:

Have I you	
Has he, has she	lost it?
Have we etc.	

SPECIAL POINTS TO NOTE

We use the Present Perfect

a to talk about things that have or haven't happened

▷ *Examples:* **I've lost** *my passport.*
I haven't found *it yet.*
Helen has had *her baby.*

b to talk about experiences

▷ *Examples: Have you ever eaten snails?*
I've never eaten snails myself.
He's been to Hong Kong but he's never been
to Japan.

But we **never** use the Present Perfect when the time is mentioned or implied. As soon as the time is mentioned, we use the Simple Past tense.

▷ *Example: Have you ever visited Athens?*
Yes, we spent a month there last year.

F LISTENING

PARISIAN HOLIDAY

Listen to this telephone conversation between Mark, who is visiting Paris with a friend, and his sister, Rosie, who lives in Chester. Then make a list of the things Mark has done and the things he tells his sister he hasn't done.

UNIT
10

G WRITING ACTIVITY

WRITING A LETTER

Listen again to the conversation between Rosie and Mark. Imagine you are visiting an English speaking country — England, the USA, Canada, or Australia.

Write a letter to a friend, telling him/her about some of the things you have done/seen during your visit and some of the things you are going to do.

Check the reading text for unit 9, for the correct layout of an English letter.
Write between 100 and 150 words.

Test 2

1 USE A FORM OF THE WORK IN BRACKETS TO COMPLETE THE FOLLOWING SENTENCES.

▷ *Example: A _____ novel usually has a happy ending. (romance)*
*A **romantic** novel usually has a happy ending.*

1 The Scottish wildcat is a very _____ animal. (aggression)
2 Billiards isn't a very _____ game. (energy)
3 I don't think that's a _____ answer to my question. (satisfaction)
4 They publish _____ books. (religion)
5 Be careful what you say to her. She's very _____ . (sense)
6 'Get out,' she shouted _____ . (anger)
7 Very _____ he picked up the china dog and looked underneath. (care)
8 It wasn't an _____ game. (excitement)
9 The weather here is _____ hot at the moment. (terror)
10 She looked _____ at the photograph. (sadness)

10 Marks

2 WRITE A SENTENCE SAYING <u>HOW LONG AGO</u> EACH OF THESE THINGS HAPPENED.

▷ *Example: (Assume it is Friday) you went shopping on Wednesday.*
*You write: I went shopping **two days ago.***

1 You went to the hairdresser last week.
2 The President died in 1980.
3 You went on holiday last August.
4 Your grandfather bought the house when he was a very young man.
5 You saw Peter last Sunday.

(5 Marks)

UNIT

10

3 WRITE FIVE SENTENCES ABOUT THINGS YOU HAVE OR HAVEN'T DONE.

▷ Example: New York.
  I've visited New York or **I haven't visited** New York.

1 Australia
2 roast beef
3 a horse
4 an aeroplane
5 coca cola

5 Marks

4 PUT THE VERBS IN THE PASSAGE BELOW INTO THE PRESENT PERFECT TENSE OR THE SIMPLE PAST TENSE.

When I decided to go to Spain for my holiday this year, I (not expect) to meet too many English people. But as soon as I (arrive) at the airport I (know) that I had made a mistake. The airport (be) absolutely full of English people, all going to Spain. Well, I (enjoy) my holiday. I (lie) on the golden sand and (swim) in the clear blue sea, but wherever I (go) I (hear) people speaking English. So next year I (decide) to go somewhere completely different. I'm going to Russia.

10 Marks

5 YOU ARE ON HOLIDAY IN SCOTLAND. USE THE NOTES BELOW TO WRITE A SHORT LETTER TO YOUR FRIEND JOHN.

21 Drummond Place,
Edinburgh,
Scotland
20th July

Dear John,

1 We/arrive/Edinburgh/last Sunday.
2 We/have/very/nice/time.
3 We/stay/fashionable part/Edinburgh.
4 In fact/our hotel/near/centre/city.
5 Yesterday/coach trip/Loch Lomond.
6 Scenery/beautiful.
7 Unfortunately/forget/bring/camera/with me.
8 But/buy/new one/tomorrow/in Edinburgh.
9 Next week/we/go/the Highlands/few days.
10 I/take/a lot/photographs.

All good wishes,

(You sign it)

20 Marks
Total Marks: 50

UNIT

10

4 Brick Lane
Plymouth
Devonshire
10th March

Dear Sonia,

Thanks for writing. I'm sorry I haven't found time to answer your letter before now, but we've all been ever so busy.

Important things have been happening at school. Heidi and Sarah have end of term tests coming up soon, so they've been working quite hard. Tom and I have been trying to help them with their reading and number work. Heidi enjoys school very much, but I'm afraid Sarah sometimes finds it difficult to concentrate.

I think I mentioned to you that the two girls now go to a dancing class on Saturday mornings. Great excitement, next week they are performing in a show at the local theatre. So I have been busy making costumes – two sugar plum fairies and two Mary Poppins outfits.

You say in your letter that you are going to Morocco for your summer holiday. I'm afraid we have only just started thinking about ours. Tom brought home a pile of brochures yesterday. We might go to Jersey.

Love to all the family,

Jenny.

Reading

A WHAT KIND OF LETTER IS THIS?

UNIT

11

66

COMPREHENSION QUESTIONS

1 Does Jenny go to school?
2 Who is Tom?
3 Who are Sarah and Heidi?
4 How old do you think they are?
5 What has Jenny been helping the girls to do?
6 What has she been making?
7 What have Jenny and Tom just started thinking about?
8 What did Tom bring home?

B WORD BUILDING

Jenny has been making clothes for her children. Divide the following articles of clothing into three groups.

a   clothes usually worn by men
b   clothes usually worn by women
c   clothes worn by men and women

belt – blouse – bowler hat – boxer shorts – cardigan – dress – gloves – jumper – scarf – shirt – suit – sweater – tie – tights

C ANSWER THE FOLLOWING QUESTIONS, USING THE PRESENT PERFECT CONTINUOUS.

Example: Why are your shoes so muddy, Peter?
   I've been playing *football.*
   or
   *It's raining and **I've been picking** some fruit.*

1 Why are your hands so dirty, John?
2 Why is the television on?
3 Why has Harold got his camera with him?
4 Why are that lady's eyes so red?
5 Why is the slide projector standing in the middle of the room?
6 Why is the jar of instant coffee on the kitchen table?
7 Why is your car parked on this yellow line, Madam?
8 Why is that dictionary not in its proper place on the bookshelf?
9 Why are those records not in their sleeves?
10 Why are those people coming out of the cinema blinking their eyes?

D LOOK AT THIS SITUATION

Clare types well. She has just removed a letter from the typewriter.
She's been typing a letter.

Study the following situations and make similar sentences:

UNIT

11

1 Gary is three years old. He has an orange mark around his mouth and there is an empty bottle of orange juice beside him.

2 There is a smell of cigarette smoke in the changing room. The sports teacher is not happy about this.

3 Tony left home later than usual and arrived at the station just in time to catch the train. He is perspiring.

4 Sheila has a friend called Dick. She has just put the phone down. So has Dick.

5 John sat near the radio while the news was on. He has just turned it off.

6 Young Fred fell over and hurt his knee. He's OK now, but there are tear marks beneath his eyes.

7 Ken and Louise are wearing swimsuits. They are sitting on the beach. They are drying their bodies with bathing towels.

8 The kitchen ceiling looks clean and white. Mary is washing white paint from a paintbrush.

9 The dishes are draining beside the sink and Bert has just let the water in the sink run away. Now he is drying his hands.

10 While the Saturday night movie was on the television Frank and Barbara sat in front of the television set. Now the film has ended and Frank has just turned off the set.

Exercise

E THIS EXERCISE IS DESIGNED TO HELP YOU TO KNOW WHEN TO SAY <u>I'VE DONE IT</u> AND WHEN TO SAY <u>I'VE BEEN DOING IT</u>.

Study the following situations and decide what to say:

1 It is breakfast time. You are sitting in the hotel restaurant waiting for a friend. You had your breakfast half an hour ago and the waitress has cleared away the dishes. Another waitress approaches and says: 'What would you like for breakfast?'

2 You are a little late for an appointment. Your hair is clean, but rather damp. Your friend wants to know why you are late.

3 You can't find your glasses. A friend sees you trying to read the paper without them and says: 'Why aren't you wearing your glasses?'

4 You enjoy baking and there is a fruit cake in the oven. A friend comments on the fact that you look rather warm.

5 Your friend suggests that you should go to a film with him/her. You saw the film some time ago and didn't like it.

UNIT

11

6 There was a problem with the car, but you have put the matter right. Your hands are covered in oil and a friend comments on this fact.

7 All your friends are talking about a new record. You heard it on the radio twice yesterday and again this morning. A friend says: 'You must come and listen to it. It's great.'

8 It's been very hot at night recently and in weather like this you have difficulty in sleeping well. A friend says you look tired.

9 Yesterday you couldn't find your cheque book, but this morning it turned up. A friend says: 'What have you done about your cheque book?'

10 When you saw the choc-ice in the refrigerator you couldn't resist it. A little later your friend opens the fridge and says 'I thought there was one choc-ice left.'

NOTE HOW WE FORM THE **PRESENT PERFECT CONTINUOUS**

Statements:

I've He's	been watching	a play on television.

Negatives:

I haven't He hasn't	been watching	the news.

Questions:

Have you Has he	been watching	the news?

SPECIAL POINTS TO NOTE

The Present Perfect Continuous tense is used for an action that started in the past and

a is still continuing.

▷ *Example: Look, do you see that policeman? He's been standing there all the morning.*

You don't have Tom's telephone number, do you? I've been trying to find it in the telephone directory.

b has finished very recently. In this case some result of the action can often be observed.

▷ *Example: You look hot.*
Yes, we've been playing tennis.

I'm not crying. I've been peeling onions.

Note: For Present Perfect with since and for see Unit 15.

F LISTENING

A NEW FLAT

You are going to hear a telephone conversation. Before you listen to the tape, study the following vocabulary:

compact:	close together, filling a small space
tiny:	very small
junk:	rubbish or things not being used at present
state:	condition
work surface:	flat area suitable for cutting up food or peeling vegetables
sale:	when there is a sale, goods are offered at reduced prices
midget:	very small person

Listen to the telephone conversation between Monica and Debbie and answer these questions:

1 Do you think Debbie and Monica are a) friends b) relations c) colleagues who work together?
2 Do you think Monica goes out to work? If so, what do you think her job might be?
3 Do you think Debbie goes out to work? If so, what do you think her job might be?

Listen to the tape again, several times if necessary, and find out:

4 what Peter has been doing.
5 what Monica has been doing.
6 what Debbie has been doing.
7 what Monica is planning to do.

Finally,

8 Write a short description of the flat, giving as much detail as possible.

Writing

G WRITING ACTIVITY

COMPLETE THE TELEPHONE CONVERSATION

Your friend Rolf, with whom you share a flat, is staying at a seaside hotel. He telephones you and asks you to send him some cassettes.

Below is the beginning of the dialogue that takes place. Write out the complete dialogue. Remember to ask Rolf what he has been doing during his holiday.

You: 237 4591
Rolf: Hello, this is Rolf. Do you think you could do something for me?
You: _____
Rolf: I left a little pile of cassettes on the table beside my bed. Do you think you could post them to me?
You: _____

UNIT
11

JOINING THE CLUB

A WHAT KIND OF CLUB IS THE WRITER TALKING ABOUT?

As I turned the corner at the end of my road, I came upon a learner driver practising his three-point turn, The instructor waved me by and I felt sorry for him. What a way to earn your bread and butter! But I felt even sorrier for the learner driver.

When you can drive, it's as easy as riding a bicycle, but when you can't, it's impossibly difficult. There are so many things you have to remember to do at the same time: look in the mirror, give your signal, do this with your left foot, do that with your right foot. Now it's time to look in the mirror again. You move forward, jerkily, a yard or two and then realise that you still have the handbrake on.

It's even worse when you get into a stream of traffic. The lights turn red. You pull up. The lights turn green again. You move forward then stall the engine. Irate drivers behind you honk their horns in fury. The lights turn red. Your hands are shaking and your heart is beating and your throat is dry.

Finally, after many lessons, you pass your test. You think you can drive. For the first time you set off alone in your vehicle. But why do all the other drivers want to drive faster than you? That huge lorry behind you; surely it's closer than necessary. Your eye catches the temperature gauge. Isn't the engine warmer than it should be? When did you check the water? And when did you last fill up with petrol?

But all bad things come to an end. One day, a few months later, you are sitting in a queue of traffic and you find yourself muttering unkind things about some less experienced driver than yourself. You realise with astonishment that you are, at last, a member of the club. You really have learnt to drive.

UNIT

12

COMPREHENSION QUESTIONS

1 Why did the instructor wave the writer by?
2 Who did the writer feel sorrier for, the learner or the instructor?
3 Why must you look in your mirror from time to time?
4 Why do other drivers sound their horns if you stall your engine?
5 Explain what the writer means by· **You think you can drive**.
6 What is it that makes you realise suddenly that you really **can** drive?

B WORD BUILDING

Match the following **driving expressions** with the likely **reasons** for taking these actions.

a) sound your horn   b) put out your left hand indicator   c) put your foot on the brakes   d) put your foot down on the accelerator   e) look in your mirror   f) take off your handbrake   g) look at the petrol gauge   h) glance at your speedometer   i) change a wheel   j) clean your windscreen

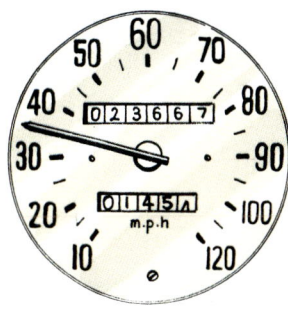

1 You want to slow down.
2 You are about to move off.
3 You want to increase your speed.
4 You intend to turn left.
5 You wish to check that you have enough fuel.
6 You can't see where you are going.
7 You wish to attract someone's attention.
8 You probably have a puncture.
9 You want to check how fast you're going.
10 You need to see what's behind you.

C WE FORM COMPARATIVES BY ADDING -ER TO SHORT ADJECTIVES.

▷ *Examples: She was **smaller than** her husband.*
*He is **kinder than** she is.*

Make similar comparisons about the following sentences:

1 How ripe the apples and pears were.
2 How fast the Porsche and the Renault are.
3 How tasty the chicken soup and the vegetable soup were.
4 How fresh the fish is at the seaside and in the city.
5 How old the castle and the cathedral are.
6 How clear the view was yesterday and is today.
7 How sweet the black cherries and the red cherries are.
8 How young Edmund and his sister look.
9 How brave you were and he was.
10 How heavy John and Mary's luggage was.

UNIT

12

Exercise

D WE FORM THE COMPARATIVE OF LONGER ADJECTIVES AND ADVERBS WITH <u>MORE</u>.

▷ *Examples: These chairs are* **more comfortable than** *the ones upstairs.*
I watch television **more frequently than** *I used to.*

Make similar sentences:

1 Say which lesson you found more interesting at school, history or biology.
2 Which do you think is more dangerous, water-skiing or motor racing?
3 Who do you think drives more dangerously, Tom or Jim?
4 Which journey did you find more tiring, the one from Rio to London, or the one from London to Hong Kong?
5 Who do you think are more excitable, Spaniards or Italians?
6 Which game do you think is more exciting, tennis or football?
7 Which do you think is the more expensive city, New York or Paris?
8 Say who you think runs his department more efficiently, Mr Brown or Mr Green.
9 Which is the more convenient way of paying a bill, to pay by cash or to pay by cheque?
10 Who do you think behaved more sensibly after the ship hit the rocks, the passengers who waited to be rescued or those who tried to swim ashore?

Exercise

E THE OPPOSITE OF <u>MORE THAN</u> IS <u>LESS THAN</u> AND WE CAN EXPRESS SIMILAR IDEAS USING <u>NOT</u> . . . <u>AS</u> . . . <u>AS</u>.

▷ *Example: Tom earns £60 a week. Fred earns £65 a week.*
Tom earns **less than** *Fred.*
or *Tom doesn't earn* **as much as** *Fred.*

Make sentences with <u>less than</u> or <u>as . . . as</u>:

1 Mary's flat cost £40,000. June's flat only cost £35,000.
2 Mr Brown weighs 60 kilos. His wife weighs 65 kilos.
3 Philip and Harriet are both eight months old. Philip cries a lot more than Harriet.
4 On average Harriet sleeps for 16 hours out of each 24. Philip only sleeps for about 13 hours.
5 Mrs Black listens to the radio all day, but Mr Black goes out to work. So he only listens at breakfast time.

6 Charles likes a big meal in the evening. His wife Louise doesn't eat a lot.

7 John paid £1,000 for his secondhand car. Fred only paid £950 for his.

8 Frank and his father both like a game of tennis. Frank's father is retired and he plays most days. But Frank only plays at weekends.

9 David and Elaine are twins, but they're very different. David talks a lot, while Elaine is rather silent.

10 However David usually has a worried look on his face, while Elaine often smiles to herself.

NOTE HOW WE FORM COMPARATIVES

We add -er to short adjectives and adverbs.

▷ *Examples:* Trudy is **smaller than** *her sister.*
She swims **faster than** *her brother.*

We use <u>more</u> with longer adjectives and adverbs.

▷ *Examples: The men's singles tennis final was* **more exciting** *than it was last year.*
I thought she sang even **more beautifully** *than she did last time.*

The opposite of <u>more than</u> is <u>less than</u>.

▷ *Example: She eats* **less than** *I do.*

When comparing things or people, we often use as . . . as

▷ *Examples: The Lotus isn't* **as fast as** *the Ferrari.*
Henderson drove nearly **as dangerously as** *his team mate.*

Learn these irregular comparisons carefully:

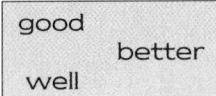

That was a **good** film on the television yesterday, but the one this evening should be even **better**.
John did **well** in the exam, but his brother did even **better**: He got 95%.

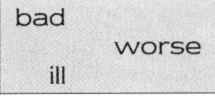

That morning there was **bad** news on radio, but **worse** was to come.
It was obvious that Pete was very **ill**. That evening he was **worse**.

UNIT

12

Listening

F LISTENING

UNDERSTANDING ENGLISH

Listen to this extract from a broadcast about learning English. Then answer the questions below.

Before you listen to the tape, study the following vocabulary:

simplify:	make easier
counter:	long table or shelf (in a shop, for instance)
facial:	to do with the face
distorted:	changed, made to sound different
VHF:	very high frequency
available:	obtainable, people can get them
specialist bookshop:	bookshop that specialises or deals especially in certain types of book
get hold of:	obtain
dub:	record
Turkish sound track:	Turkish voices speaking in the Turkish language
subtitles:	words spoken by the actors translated into another language and printed over the picture

Answer the first three questions when you have listened to the tape once.

1 Where does Mahmut come from?
2 Where does he work?
3 What is his problem?

Listen to the tape again, several times if necessary. Then answer these questions:

4 Linda suggests three reasons why a foreigner might find it difficult to understand an English person speaking English. What are they?
5 What is the other interesting point about listening and understanding that Peter makes?
6 What happens to someone's voice on the telephone?
7 Would it be easier to understand the news on television or on the radio?
8 The speakers suggest three ways in which Mahmut might practise listening to English. What are they?

Listen to the tape once more.

9 During the discussion, the various speakers use the comparative form a number of times. Write down six examples.

G WRITING ACTIVITY

MAKING COMPARISONS

Write about living in a city and living in a village.

Compare: the choice of shops, the traffic (pollution), the things you can do (entertainment), the people and anything else you want to mention.

Finish with a conclusion, like this:

Personally I prefer to live in . . . because . . .

You will need between 80 and 130 words.

77

UNIT
12

Reading

A WHICH COUNTRY GAVE US THE FIRST TV PROGRAMME?

Nowadays we take it for granted that when we come home from work we can turn on the television and find out what has been happening in the world. We forget, sometimes, that both television and home video are comparatively recent inventions.

In 1935 a German television station began transmitting programmes from Berlin, but the picture quality was disappointing. A year later, in 1936, the first high definition television broadcasting service started in London. At that time there were only about a hundred television sets in the country and as they were very expensive, only the wealthiest families could afford one.

It was not until 1962 that the earliest transatlantic transmission was made, the pictures being bounced off the satellite Telstar 1. A year later, in 1963, the first public demonstration of a home video recorder took place.

Since the early days of television, advertising has provided much of the finance necessary to run television stations throughout the world. The highest sum ever paid to advertise on television was the 555,000 dollars per half minute during breaks in the transmission of the Super Bowl, the big American football championship final.

Up until the present time, however, the most popular broadcast, or rather that watched by the greatest number of viewers, has been the Live Aid concert organised by Bob Geldof. On this occasion twelve satellites were used to bring the programme to more than a billion people all over the world.

COMPREHENSION QUESTIONS

1 Why did poor families not have a television in 1936?
2 How many sets were there in England in 1936?
3 Compare the quality of the pictures sent out by the British and German stations.
4 How were pictures sent across the Atlantic in 1962?
5 How old is the video recorder?
6 From what source does much of the finance for television programmes come?
7 What exactly did advertisers pay 555,000 dollars for?
8 Explain why Bob Geldof needed 12 satellites. Did you watch?

Exercise

B WORD BUILDING

We **turn on** the television, the light, or the oven. But '**turn**' is used together with various other prepositions to form useful phrasal verbs:

turn back   turn down   turn in   turn into   turn off
turn out   turn over   turn up.

Use your dictionary and choose verbs from this list to complete the story below:

John searched everywhere for the kitten, but she didn't ____1____. As he was feeling very tired, he decided to ____2____. He ____3____ the lights and went upstairs. He washed, ____4____ the covers on the bed and climbed in. But although he felt tired, he could not sleep. The thought that they had ____5____ his application to become a policeman still annoyed him. Then he thought he heard a scratching sound. He ____6____ on to his side and listened. There it was again. He switched on the bedside lamp, got out of bed and opened the wardrobe. The kitten looked up at him, blinking in the sudden light. 'Oh, so that's where you got to', said John.

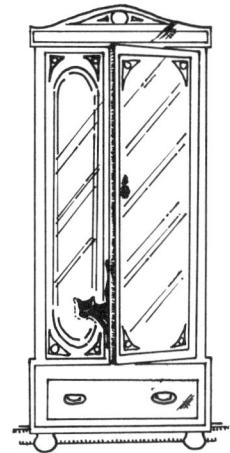

C SAY WHICH IS <u>THE BIGGEST</u>, <u>THE SMALLEST</u>, <u>THE MOST EXPENSIVE</u>, ETC.

1 My fish weighed 1kg, Tom's weighed 1.5kg and Dick's weighed 2kg.
2 John's car cost £4,900, Peter's cost £4,200 and Frank's cost £900.
3 The journey to Paris took 1 hour. The journey to Malaga took 2½ hours, but the journey to Rio took more than 12 hours.
4 In the plane accident at Manchester 23 people died. In the accident at Dublin, 10 people were killed, but in the Detroit accident 104 people lost their lives.
5 Mr Brown is 22. Mr Green is 24. Mr Black is 26. All the other teachers are at least 30 years old.
6 In the last 10 years 12 people have died trying to climb the east face of the Vogelspitz mountain. In the same period 6 people have lost their lives climbing the north face and 2 climbing the south face.

D WE FORM THE SUPERLATIVE OF SHORT ADJECTIVES WITH <u>-EST</u>, BUT WE USE <u>MOST</u> WITH LONG ADJECTIVES.

*Examples: She is the **oldest** student in the class.*
*It was the **most exciting** game I've ever seen.*

Make more superlative statements.

1 It hasn't rained as much any day this year as it did yesterday. (wet)
2 I haven't read such an interesting book for a long time. (interesting)
3 None of the chairs in this room are more comfortable than this one. (comfortable)
4 Simon is wealthier than either of his two brothers. (wealthy)
5 I have never taken a harder exam. (hard)
6 She never made a more difficult decision. (difficult)
7 He enjoyed the party more than any party he could remember. (enjoyable)
8 You've never driven a faster car. (fast)
9 It's a long time since I saw such a critical report. (critical)
10 Charles has never had a more understanding boss. (understanding)

E JOIN TOGETHER THE TWO PARTS OF THE DIALOGUES BELOW TO MAKE EIGHT SENSIBLE CONVERSATIONS. YOU WILL THEN FIND THAT YOU HAVE TWO SPARE RESPONSES. COMPLETE THE LAST TWO

DIALOGUES BY INVENTING SUITABLE OPENINGS.

Openings	Responses
1 It must be lovely there.	Yes, I think he's probably the longest serving member of staff.
2 Charles is looking smart.	Probably that one beside the window.
3 Where did the finest porcelain come from originally?	I'm afraid these are the cheapest we have in stock.
4 Those shoes look comfortable.	Does she go out to work?
5 It's certainly the most attractive house we've seen.	Have you looked at many?
6 I think she's the rudest woman I've ever met.	They're a special wide fitting, but I had the most awful trouble finding them.
7 I'm looking for some knives and forks, but I don't want to pay too much for them.	From China, I would imagine.
8 Which is the most valuable painting in the gallery?	Yes, it's the most beautiful country I've ever visited.
	Yes, it fits nicely.
	Yes, he's wearing his best suit.

NOTE HOW WE FORM SUPERLATIVES

We add -est to short adjectives.

▷ *Examples: He was the **youngest** of the children.*
*It was the **hottest** summer anyone could remember.*

We use most with long adjectives.

▷ *Examples:* **Three men in a boat** *was far and away* Jerome's **most successful** *book.*
*It was the **most remarkable** performance I've ever seen.*

81

UNIT
13

The opposite of <u>most</u> is <u>least</u>.

▷ *Example: This must be the* **least reliable** *bus service in Europe.*

The superlative of <u>good</u> is <u>best</u>.

▷ *Example: They were the* **best** *shoes I could buy for the price.*

The superlative of <u>bad</u> and <u>ill</u> is <u>worst</u>.

▷ *Example: It was the* **worst** *railway accident in living memory.*

F LISTENING

INTERVIEW WITH KATE EVANS: TELEVISION REPORTER

You are going to hear an interview between Martin Wright and Kate Evans who is a well-known television reporter. Before you listen to the tape, study the following vocabulary:

fascinating:	very interesting
assignment:	job given to a person
struggling:	fighting
intact:	in one piece
debris:	loose bricks or pieces of stone
concrete:	mixture of cement, sand and stones
bruised:	injured by a blow, so that the flesh may turn blue
incredible:	almost impossible to believe
hang around:	wait
kippers:	smoked herrings
starve:	suffer from a lack of food
dangle:	hang suspended
vertical:	straight

Listen to the tape and say what was Kate's

— most dangerous assignment,
— most interesting assignment,
— most exciting assignment,
— saddest assignment,
— most frightening assignment,
— most boring assignment.

Then listen to the tape again, several times if necessary and answer these questions:

1 Why was Beirut a particularly dangerous place to be?
2 Describe how Kate was injured while she was there.
3 What did Pete have to do?
4 Explain what Kate found exciting about the assignment in Kenya.
5 What problem did the people in Ethiopia have?
6 What was it about the assignment in the north of England that particularly scared Kate?

G WRITING ACTIVITY

THE MOST EXCITING DAY OF MY LIFE

Write between 100 and 150 words on: **The most exciting day of my life — so far.**

UNIT

13

AN UNWISE CHOICE

A WHY SHOULDN'T YOU GO BY FIRST IMPRESSIONS?

One shouldn't always go by first impressions. In my home town there lived a giant of a man with huge hands and a manner so fierce and unfriendly that he always sat alone in any public place. Yet to those who knew him, he was a kind and generous friend. In the same way one should never assume that somebody who looks inoffensive is always going to behave in an inoffensive manner.

Recently my young brother, who works for a famous American airline, was reminded of this truth. The plane was overbooked and for once all the passengers turned up. So my brother had the difficult task of choosing three passengers and informing them that they couldn't travel on the flight in question.

Knowing that the young are generally impatient and often aggressive, my brother chose three elderly travellers, an English couple and a little old American lady.

The English couple accepted the situation and went to have a drink while waiting for the next flight. Then my brother approached the American lady, whose name was Mrs Pepper, with a sad smile on his face. 'Mrs Pepper? May I have a few words? I'm afraid we have a problem.'

'A problem? What do you mean, we have a problem, young man?' 'Would you like to come into the office?' asked my brother, sensing that this was not going to be easy.

'Oh, very well, but only for a moment. I have a plane to catch, you know.' 'Er . . . yes.' My brother explained the position.

The little lady looked at him with steely, blue eyes. 'Young man,' she said, 'I don't believe you are aware that you are talking to Mrs Katherine Pepper, widow of General Arnold Pepper, of the United States Army Air Force and I'd like to inform you, further, that the President of your airline was a personal friend of the General's. In the circumstances I'd advise you to sort this out right away, otherwise you're going to be in a lot of trouble. Do I make myself clear?'

'Yes, Ma'am,' replied my brother.

COMPREHENSION QUESTIONS

1 Explain why the big man always sat alone.
2 Why were three passengers unable to travel on the flight?
3 Why did this cause a problem for the writer's brother?
4 Explain why the writer's brother selected older passengers.
5 How did the English couple react?
6 Explain why the writer's brother invited Mrs Pepper to step into the office.
7 Explain the term: **steely blue eyes**. What did the writer's brother know, as soon as she looked at him with them?

DISCUSSION. WORK IN PAIRS.

In choosing the American lady, the writer's brother obviously made a mistake. Explain exactly why. (You should be able to think of **three** reasons.)

What do think happened next?
Did anything like this ever happen to you?
How would you react in similar circumstances?

UNIT

14

B WORD BUILDING

Mrs Pepper was fairly **aggressive**. The noun form of
aggressive is **aggression**. The adverb is **aggressively**.

Work with a partner. Use your dictionary and
complete the table below:

	Noun	Adjective	Adverb
	aggression	aggressive	aggressively
1		arrogant	
2	conceit		
3			desperately
4	help		
5		intelligent	
6	optimist		
7			pessimistically
8		skilful	
9			stupidly
10	thought		

C NOTICE HOW WE CAN ASK AND ANSWER QUESTIONS ABOUT PREFERENCES, USING LIKE.

 *Examples: Which **would you like**, tea or coffee?*
I'd like *coffee, please.*

Would you like to *visit the town this
afternoon, or go to the beach?*
I'd like to *visit the town.*

Answer the questions.

1 Which would you like, brown bread or white?
2 Would you like to go to the zoo or to the museum
tomorrow?
3 Would you like to watch television or go for a walk?
4 Which would you like to drink, tea or orange juice?
5 Where would you like to go this afternoon, into the
country or along the coast?

**Below are the replies to five questions. You think of
the questions.**

6 I'd like cheese, please.
7 I'd like to go by train.
8 I'd like to leave in the morning.
9 I'd like a piece of cake, please.
10 I'd like to have dinner in the hotel.

D WE CAN USE SHOULD AND SHOULDN'T TO GIVE ADVICE.

 *Examples: I think you should see a doctor about your
headaches.
You shouldn't walk home alone so late.*

Give your friend advice:

1 Your friend has a bad tooth.
2 Your friend smokes 30 cigarettes a day.
3 Your friend drives faster than you think is sensible.
4 Your friend gets up very late every morning.
5 You think your friend is too generous with his/her money.
6 You don't think your friend writes often enough to his/her parents.
7 Your friend seems to live on hamburgers and coca cola.
8 Your friend's eyes are watery and he/she has problems reading small print.
9 Your friend doesn't enjoy his/her job at all.
10 Your friend never gets to bed till 1 a.m. or 2 a.m. and always looks tired in the morning.

E MAY AND MIGHT ARE OFTEN USED TO ASK PERMISSION TO DO SOMETHING IN A RATHER FORMAL WAY.

▷ *Example:* **May I** *watch the athletics on the television?*
Yes, of course.
or
I'm afraid the TV isn't working.

Work in pairs. Ask for and give or refuse permission in the following situations.

1 To borrow a car.
2 To see some photographs.
3 To have a key.
4 To look at someone's programme.
5 To have a clean towel.
6 To look at somebody's newspaper.
7 To use someone's telephone.
8 To listen to the news on someone's radio.

Can you think of two more situations where May I or Might I would be useful?

SPECIAL POINTS TO NOTE

Would you like (to) . . . is a common way of inviting people to eat, drink, visit, etc.
I'd like (to) . . . is the usual polite way of expressing the want idea.

▷ *Examples:* **Would you like to** *come to a barbecue on Saturday evening?*
I'd like to *come, but I must check with Jennie first.*

Should and **shouldn't** are useful when we want to offer advice or comment on whether it is wise or not to carry out some course of action.

▷ *Examples:* **You shouldn't** *leave that door unlocked.*

There's something wrong with that tape. **You should** *take it back to the shop where you bought it.* **They should** *block up the end of this road, then drivers couldn't use it as a short cut.*

May and **Might** are often used when we want to ask permission to do something in rather a formal way.

▷ *Examples: May I have the key to the shed, please?*
Might I make a suggestion?

Note: In both these examples it is possible to use **Can** instead of **May** and **Might**. The sense would remain the same, but the style would be more informal.

F LISTENING

A sweet tooth

You are going to hear an extract from a radio programme in which listeners talk to the radio doctor. Before you listen to the tape, study the following vocabulary.

overweight:	too heavy
ever so fat:	very fat
lack of energy:	shortage of energy, absence of energy
keen on:	enthusiastic about
consume:	eat
damage:	harm
spare time:	free time
leaflet	small printed sheet

Listening

a Listen to the tape several times if necessary and decide whether the following statements are true, or false, or whether we don't have enough information to say.

1 Ethel is ringing the doctor because she's worried about her health.
2 Ethel's husband is more than 40 years old.
3 Ethel's husband weighs more than he should.
4 Ethel enjoys cooking.
5 Ethel's husband enjoys cooking.
6 Ethel's husband sometimes makes cakes.
7 Ethel believes her husband eats too much sugar.
8 Ethel is silly to worry about her husband's health.
9 Ethel works at the post office.
10 Ethel's husband occasionally watches television.

b What does the doctor want Ethel to do?
What will he then do?
Explain why the doctor suggests doing this.

c Listen to the tape again, more than once if necessary, and find one example of the use of **Would you like**, two examples of **I'd like**, one example of **shouldn't**, two examples of **May I** and one example of **Might I**.
Write down the sentences in which you hear each of these expressions.

G WRITING ACTIVITY

SHOULD/SHOULDN'T

Imagine you work for the tourist board in your own country. You are asked to produce a leaflet advising visitors to look after their private property carefully.

Try and think of up to 10 **shoulds** and **shouldn'ts**.

You might begin like this:

ADVICE TO FOREIGN VISITORS

1 You should never leave your luggage unattended in a public place.
2 . . .

▷ # A LETTER FROM PRISON ◁

Dear Mum and Dad,

I am afraid this letter will come as a bit of a shock to you, particularly as I have not written for some time. As you can see from the address at the top of the letter, I am in prison on remand. I have been here since last Friday. Unfortunately the auditors have discovered that some money is missing from the branch of the bank where I have been working for the last six months.

Just after I arrived here, the bank introduced a new, computerised system for handling customers' accounts. As you know, I have been interested in computers since my schooldays, so I found it easy to learn to operate the new system, while some of the staff who have worked here for quite a long time, had problems.

Apparently somebody has been "milking" customers' accounts; that is transferring money out of customers' accounts, without the customer knowing about it. A very large sum is involved and they have accused me because I am a comparatively new member of staff. I have been using the computer more than anybody else and they say they have evidence against me. Of course, it is all a dreadful mistake. Either the money is not really missing at all, or somebody else is guilty.

Please do not worry.

Much love to you both, Ralph.

Reading

A WHY IS RALPH IN PRISON?

COMPREHENSION QUESTIONS

1 How long has Ralph been in prison?
2 When did he last write to his parents?
3 What have the auditors found out?
4 How long has Ralph worked at the bank?
5 Why did he find it so easy to learn to operate the new system?
6 Why do you think older members of staff often find it difficult to learn to operate a new, computerised system?
7 What do the auditors believe has been happening?
8 Why do they think that Ralph is the person responsible?

DISCUSSION

Work in pairs. Read the letter again. Do you think Ralph is guilty or not guilty?
What do you think is going to happen next?
Work as a class. How many students believe Ralph is guilty?
Explain why you think so.
Who thinks Ralph is not guilty? Explain why.

UNIT
15

90

B WORD BUILDING

Ralph is in prison. He is waiting to appear in court. Study the list of words and expressions below. They are all connected with the law. You may use your dictionary. Then, choosing suitable words and phrases from the list, to fill the gaps, write out the story.

barrister – solicitor – case – oath – cells – dock – prosecution – defence – judge – jury – witness – evidence – guilty – not guilty

They woke me early and brought me to the ____1____ below the court. Then about 10 o'clock they took me upstairs and put me in the ____2____. I noticed my ____3____, sitting in front of me. He turned and smiled. Then we all had to stand and the ____4____ entered. A tall ____5____ for the ____6____ outlined the ____7____ against me. Fortunately, however, I had two reliable ____8____ who were able to convince the ____9____ that my story was true and I was found ____10____.

C WE CAN SAY: RALPH HAS BEEN WORKING AT THE BANK FOR SIX MONTHS.

MAKE MORE SENTENCES LIKE THIS:

1 Sybil and John are sitting in the restaurant. The waiter took their order 10 minutes ago.
2 Mr Parker smokes 20 cigarettes a day. He smoked his first cigarette when he was 16. Now he's 46.
3 Ivor Allen wrote his first detective story 12 years ago. He writes a new one every year.
4 Tom Elliot breeds prize pigs. He started when he was 25. Now he's 45.
5 The runners in the marathon race set off at 6 p.m. It's 6.30 p.m. and they're still running.
6 Frieda Schultz learnt to play the violin when she was 8 years old. She became a music teacher. Now she's 88 years old and she still plays occasionally.

D WE CAN SAY: RALPH HAS WORKED AT THE BANK SINCE JANUARY.

MAKE MORE SENTENCES LIKE THIS:

1 Mr and Mrs Curtis live in Jersey. They went to live there in 1970.
2 Peter is an actor. He became an actor when he left school.
3 Dr Rogers started to collect stamps when he was a little boy. He still collects stamps.
4 Tony is interested in computers. He first became interested in computers when his father bought one.
5 Mrs Banks has an account with Bulgin's Bank. She first opened an account there in 1965.
6 Old Mrs Dickson feels rather lonely now. You see, her husband died.

UNIT
15

Exercise

E STUDY THESE PATTERNS:

He came to Paris three months ago.
He's been in Paris for three months.

He joined the firm last January.
He's worked for the firm since last January.

Finish each of the following sentences so that it means the same as the sentence printed before it:

1 He came to work at the bank six months ago.
   He's . . .
2 They came to live in the house next door last June.
   They've . . .
3 I caught a cold last weekend and I've still got it.
   I've had . . .
4 She wrote to me two years ago, but that was the last time I heard from her.
   I haven't . . .
5 He's a soldier. He joined the army in 1982.
   He's . . .
6 These spots appeared on my chest a week ago and they're still there.
   I've had . . .
7 She lives in Nice. She moved there in 1979.
   She's . . .
8 He's a postman. He became a postman three years ago.
   He's . . .
9 He joined the police force in 1984 and he's still a policeman.
   He's . . .
10 He came out of prison three weeks ago.
   He's . . .

SPECIAL POINTS TO NOTE

We use the Present Perfect (or the Present Perfect Continuous) + <u>since</u> with a point in time.

▷ *Examples: I've worked at the bank **since January**.*
*They've been living in Jersey **since 1980**.*
*He's been interested in computers **since he left school**.*

We use the Present Perfect (or the Present Perfect Continuous) + <u>for</u> with a length in time.

▷ *Examples: I've worked at the bank **for six months**.*
*They've been living in Jersey **for ten years**.*
*He's been interested in computers **for a very long time**.*

Note: We only use the Present Perfect tenses when the thing we are talking about is still happening, or occasionally when it was happening until a very short while ago.

We sometimes use the Simple Past tense with **for** + a length of time, when the event we are talking about took place in the past and is finished.

▷ *Example: My son speaks very good Spanish.* **He lived in Spain for two years**, *after he left university.*

F LISTENING

TROUBLE AT THE DAILY NEWS

You are going to hear an extract from a radio programme about an industrial dispute. Before you listen to the tape, study the following vocabulary:

workforce:	people who work for a company
devastating:	terrible
blow:	shock
redundancy money:	money paid to someone who loses his/her job through no fault of their own
entitled to:	have the right to
charitable institution:	organisation run for the benefit of people in need
trade union:	organisation of and for workers
negotiate:	work out
gravity:	seriousness
competition:	other companies in the same business
consequences:	results
dismiss:	sack, get rid of
grave:	place where a dead person is buried

Listen to the tape and answer the following questions:

1 Explain who Lynne Scott, Ron Freeman and Julian Frost are:
2 How long has Ron Freeman worked for the Daily News?
3 What does he say about his son?
4 Apart from sacking the workers, what has the company refused to do?
5 Listen to the tape again, several times if necessary, and make a note of the main points put forward by both Ron Freeman and Julian Frost.

G WRITING ACTIVITY

LETTER OF COMPLAINT

Refer to the notes you made on the radio discussion between Ron Freeman and Julian Frost. If necessary, listen to the tape again.

UNIT
15

Imagine you are Ron Freeman. Write a letter to the editor of the **Daily News** complaining about the way you have been treated by United Newspapers and saying what you think should happen now.

You will need between 100 and 150 words. Don't forget to put your address and the date in the top righthand corner.

Test 3

1 COMPLETE THE FOLLOWING SENTENCES WITH SINCE OR FOR:

1 He's been a member of the club – three years.
2 I haven't been home – January.
3 You've been ill – over a fortnight.
4 She hasn't seen the doctor – several months.
5 He's telephoned me three times – I got back from my holiday.

5 Marks

2 WRITE WHAT YOU WOULD SAY IN THE FOLLOWING SITUATIONS:

 Example: Somebody offers you a cup of coffee.
     You write: Oh, thank you.

1 You decide to offer somebody a cool drink.
2 You want your landlady to give you a clean towel.
3 You think your friend smokes too many cigarettes. Advise him/her to smoke fewer.
4 You are staying with English friends in their home. You want to watch the football match on the television this evening. Ask.
5 Your friend has a very bad cold. Suggest he/she sees a doctor.

5 Marks

3 PUT THE VERBS IN THE FOLLOWING SENTENCES INTO THE PRESENT PERFECT, PRESENT PERFECT CONTINUOUS OR THE SIMPLE PAST:

1 John (learn) French for three years and he still can't speak a word.
2 I (receive) a letter from my brother last week.
3 You (not tell) me yet where you're going for your holiday.
4 I (buy) the tickets yesterday.
5 We (arrive) in Spain a week ago.
6 I (not see) Iris since she got back.
7 We (spend) three very pleasant weeks in Portugal in 1986.
8 John (complain) that the weather is too hot, since we arrived in Turkey.
9 The 4th Earl (sell) the painting after his father died.
10 Yes, my sister made that pot. She (attend) a pottery class for nearly two years, now.

10 Marks

4 WRITE SENTENCES CONTAINING A COMPARATIVE OR A SUPERLATIVE.

▷ *Example: Tom's parcel weighs 4 kilos, Peter's parcel weighs 2½ kilos.*
*You write: Tom's parcel is **heavier than** Peter's **or** Peter's parcel is **lighter than** Tom's.*

Tom's parcel weighs 4 kilos, Peter's parcel weighs 2½ kilos, but Mary's parcel weighs 9 kilos.
*You write: Mary's parcel is **the heaviest or** Peter's parcel is **the lightest**.*

1 Tom is 22 years old. Peter is 21.

2 The red dress costs £20. The blue dress costs £15 and the yellow dress costs £12.

3 The church spire is 25 metres tall. The office block is 30 metres tall.

4 Motorways can be dangerous. 114 people were killed or injured on the M4 last year. In the same period 90 people were killed or injured on the M3.

5 The exams were difficult. 21 out of 25 students passed the maths exam. 17 out of 25 passed the biology exam, but only 9 out of 25 passed in physics.

6 The Jumbo jet is noisy, but the Concorde is very noisy indeed.

7 All Karen Smith's books are popular. 'Silk' sold 100,000 copies, 'Skyblue' has sold 210,000 copies so far, while 'Recognition' has sold 110,000 copies.

8 The children in the playgroup are quite young. Simon is 4. Carol is 3½ and Gary is only just 3.

9 Sarah finds the geography lessons rather boring, but the history lessons are interesting.

10 Sue bought the groceries at the cheap supermarket, but she forgot to buy the sugar. It isn't very convenient for her to go back to the supermarket. She can buy the sugar at the little shop at the end of the road for 5p more.

10 Marks

5 YOU RECEIVE A LETTER FROM A PEN-FRIEND IN ENGLAND. HER NAME IS JUNE.

She writes: . . . You have not written for over six months. No excuses now. I expect to hear from you very soon . . .

Reply to June's letter, telling her what you have been doing recently.
Write 100 – 150 words.

20 Marks

Total Marks: 50

UNIT

15

CHANGING PLACES

A WHAT DO THESE TWO PEOPLE AGREE TO DO?

It started as a joke really. Jim came home from the income tax office where he worked and Mary remarked innocently 'Hello, dear. Did you have a good day?'

'I had a terrible day,' replied Jim, crossly.

'I'm sorry,' said Mary, 'but don't blame me'.

'I don't know why I put up with it,' Jim continued.

'Well, why **do** you put up with it?' asked Mary. 'You could always change your job . . . or . . . ' and suddenly her eyes lit up . . . 'or I might go to work full-time and you can stay at home and look after the children.'

'Ha, ha and what about my pension?' enquired Jim.

'You can't spend your whole life worrying about your pension,' said Mary.

They didn't say any more about it at the time, but the idea lingered in their minds. That evening, when the children were in bed, Jim suddenly turned off the television. He looked hard at Mary. 'Do you remember what you said at tea time?'

Mary nodded. 'Do you really want to go back to work full-time?'

'I'd much rather go to work full-time myself than see you coming home in a bad mood every day,' replied Mary.

'It may not be easy,' Jim pointed out, 'you know . . me being the only father amongst all the mothers, waiting for the kids to come out of school . . . that sort of thing.'

'What **we** do is **our** business,' said Mary firmly.

Jim nodded. 'OK' he said. 'Let's give it a try and see how it works out.'

COMPREHENSION QUESTIONS

1 Where did Jim work?
2 What sort of mood was he in when he got home from work?
3 What did Mary first suggest that he might do?
4 Explain why Mary's eyes suddenly lit up.
5 What was Jim's first reaction to Mary's second suggestion?
6 Why do you think the idea lingered in their minds?
7 How do you think Mary really feels about going back to work full-time?
8 What sort of problems does Jim foresee when he says '**It may not be easy** . . .'

B WORD BUILDING

Jim is concerned about his pension. This is the money he will get when he retires. Match the following financial expressions with their definitions below:

commission – discount – dividend – earnings – income tax – insurance premium – interest – salary – VAT – wage

1 Money received by the shareholders of a company.
2 Money you have to pay if you borrow from a financial institution, or money you receive if you lend money to a financial institution.
3 Money you receive each week in exchange for your work.
4 Regular sum you pay to an insurance company.
5 Reduction in price because you pay cash, buy a large quantity, etc.
6 Money you earn.
7 Percentage of the price of the goods received by a salesman when he sells things.
8 Value added tax. A tax you pay on goods and services.
9 Tax you have to pay on the money you earn.
10 Money you receive each month in exchange for your work.

UNIT
16

C WE OFTEN USE <u>MIGHT</u> TO TELL PEOPLE ABOUT A POSSIBLE COURSE OF ACTION.

▷ *Example: Situation: You don't like your boss.*
    Possible course of action: **I might find another job.**

What might you do in the following situation?

1 Your car let you down badly last week. It broke down on the motorway.
2 You want quite a large loan.
3 You are finding the journey to your work in the city long and tiring.
4 You are wondering what to buy your sister for her birthday.
5 You are considering where to go for your summer holiday.
6 You are finding it difficult to decide what to cook this evening.
7 You had a bit of toothache last night, but this morning the tooth feels OK.
8 You heard a new record on the radio and you quite liked it.

D WE CAN USE <u>COULD</u> TO MAKE SUGGESTIONS.

▷ *Example: Your friend can't decide where to go for her holiday.*
    Suggestion: You **could** *go to Greece.*

Make more suggestions.

1 Your friend has lost weight. She has a skirt that is too big for her.
2 Your friend is unhappy about something that is going on at the school to which her children go.
3 Your friend lives in a flat and dislikes the people who live downstairs.
4 You are getting a little tired of hearing your friend complaining about articles in her daily newspaper.
5 Your friend can't decide what to buy her brother for Christmas.
6 Your friend grumbles a lot about her husband's selfishness over using the car. **She** can't drive.
7 Your friend is having problems deciding what to wear to go to a party.
8 Your friend often complains that public clocks are inaccurate or don't work. She doesn't have a watch herself.

E I'D RATHER *IS A COMMON WAY OF*
***SAYING *I'D PREFER TO*.**

▷ *Example: Do you want to visit the museum?*
            Yes, all right.
            or
            I'd rather *go and have a cup of coffee.*

Reply to the following questions.

   1 Do you want to go to the cinema?
   2 Do you want to take some photographs now?
   3 Do you want to meet my parents?
   4 Do you want to go right up to the top of the tower?
   5 Do you want to play tennis?
   6 Do you want an ice cream?
   7 Do you want to go for a swim?
   8 Do you want an apple?
   9 Do you want to take the exam in December?
  10 Do you want to look at the documents today?

SPECIAL POINTS TO NOTE

Modals such as <u>can</u>, <u>could</u>, <u>may</u>, <u>might</u> are useful for
expressing ideas about possible courses of action.

Can/could

<u>**Could**</u> is the past form of <u>**can**</u>.

▷ *Examples:* **I can** *tell him tomorrow.*
            At last **he could** *escape. (At last he was able*
            to escape)

We also use **could** to make suggestions and discuss
possibilities:

▷ *Examples: Perhaps* **you could phone him?**
            Of course, I <u>**could**</u> *change my job.*

May/might

Technically <u>**might**</u> is the past of <u>**may**</u>, but both <u>may</u>
and <u>might</u> are often used to express the idea of
possibility.

▷ *Examples: I'm afraid* **it may rain** *this evening.*
            I'm sorry you don't like George, **I might**
            marry him.

Note: <u>**may**</u> is always slightly more probable than
      <u>**might**</u>.

UNIT
16

Want to and **I'd rather** are ways of expressing wishes or preferences.

Want to

▷ *Examples:* <u>**I want to go to the zoo.**</u> *(Note that* **I'd like to go to the zoo** *is more polite)*
<u>**They want to see the penguins.**</u>

I'd rather

I'd rather is a useful way of saying **I'd prefer to.**

Note that we can use it with any person. <u>**I'd rather, he'd rather**</u>, etc.

▷ *Examples:* *Would you like to go out this evening?*
<u>**I'd rather stay at home,**</u> *if you don't mind.*

Does she want some tea?
I think <u>**she'd rather have a cool drink,**</u> *actually.*

F LISTENING

GOING INTO BUSINESS

You are going to hear a conversation between Deidre Watson and George Lucas. The conversation takes place in a local cafe, where they meet by chance.

Before you listen to the tape, study the following vocabulary:

cheer up:	look happier
gracious:	goodness
entitled to:	have the right to
redundancy money:	money paid to someone who loses their job through no fault of their own.

UNIT

16

charge the earth:	charge a lot of money
cut price:	cheap
branch out:	expand (in a new direction)
protégés:	young people who are helped in their career (usually by someone quite important)

Now listen to the conversation and answer these questions.

1 Do you think George and Deidre know one another well? Give reasons for your answers.
2 Why does Deidre open the conversation with the words 'Cheer up'?
3 What has happened?
4 Explain George's plan in your own words.
5 Listen to the tape again and make a note of two occasions when the word **might** is used.
6 Listen to the tape once more and make a note of three occasions when the word **could** is used.
7 Who uses the expression **I'd rather**? What does he/she say?

G WRITING ACTIVITY

COMPLETE THE CONVERSATION

Read the text again. Jim says: 'It may not be easy. You know, me being the only father amongst all the mothers, waiting for the kids to come out of school . . .'
Imagine Jim's son is 15 years old. Another boy asks: 'What does your Dad do?'

Jim replies: 'My Dad stays at home and looks after the house. My Mum goes out to work'.

Continue the conversation.

UNIT

16

▷ THE UNWELCOME VISITOR ◁

Reading

A WHAT HAPPENED TO LOUISE?

Louise was 72 years old and she lived by herself. The first thing she noticed when she came downstairs that Sunday morning was that her kitchen window was open. In fact it was so wide open that she had trouble shutting it. Then she realised that things were not in their proper places, finally, when she found her empty purse on the kitchen table, she realised the awful truth. At first she didn't know what to do. Then she decided to ring her son, Derek.

Derek's wife Sybil answered the phone. 'It's your mother,' she informed him, coldly. Louise told Derek about the open window, about things being in the wrong place and about the money missing from her purse.
'All right,' said Derek, 'don't touch anything. I'll be round in half an hour.'

Louise relaxed and made herself a pot of tea and some toast. Then she went from room to room wondering if anything else was missing. When Derek arrived, he was relieved to find her looking so calm. 'Have you rung the police?' he enquired. 'No? Then I'll do that straight away.' So he rang the police. As it was a Sunday, however, the police were polite, but vague. Unfortunately the only detectives on duty were out. 'We'll send someone round as soon as possible,' they said.

Derek telephoned his wife. 'I'm not sure when I'll be home, love,' he told her. 'I've got to wait for the police.' While Derek and his mother waited, Derek examined the catches on the windows and the locks on the doors. All of them were old and some of the catches hardly worked at all. Derek felt guilty. His mother was an old woman, after all. 'I'll have to change all these,' he told her.

COMPREHENSION QUESTIONS

1 Who was the unwelcome visitor?
2 Why do you think Derek doesn't live with his mother?
3 What were the three things that Louise discovered when she came downstairs that Sunday morning?
4 What three things did Derek do after he arrived at his mother's home?
5 Explain why the police didn't send someone round immediately.

Exercise

B WORD BUILDING

Below are the verb forms of ten words used in the text. Use your dictionary if necessary and write the noun form opposite each.

	Verb	Noun
1	change	
2	decide	
3	enquire	
4	examine	
5	inform	
6	realise	
7	relax	
8	relieve	
9	wait	
10	wonder	

Exercise

C DISCUSSION. WORK IN PAIRS. CONTINUE THE STORY:

Did the detectives turn up?
If so, what did they do?
What time do you think Derek got home?
What did Sybil say?
Do you think Derek changed all the locks and window catches?
What do you think Sybil said, when Derek told her about the locks and window catches?

UNIT
17

D DEREK SAYS:
I'LL BE ROUND IN HALF AN HOUR.

Go back to the text and find **three** more remarks that Derek makes, using **I'll . . .** and one that the police make, using **we'll . . .**

These are all examples of the **Simple Future**.

Study the following situations and make similar remarks:

1 Your friend is looking with interest at one of your books. You think she'd like to borrow it.
2 Your friend has written a postcard but has no stamp. You have some stamps upstairs.
3 Your friend lives five miles away and you have no car. It's late at night and it's time for her to go home.
4 Your friend says: 'Goodness, I feel quite thirsty.'
5 Your friend is filling in a form. The print is small and the room is quite dark.
6 Your friend's pen is running out of ink. She's having difficulty writing with it.
7 Your friend mentioned that she'd like to see the old Fred Astaire film that's going to be shown on television. It starts at eight o'clock and it's two minutes to eight now.
8 Your friend wants to cut out an article from the newspaper. You have some scissors in the next room.
9 You have a new record which you know your friend would like to listen to.
10 Your friend says: 'Goodness, it's a bit stuffy in this room.'

E PRACTISE MAKING PREDICTIONS WITH WILL.

▷ *Example: Your friend Anna met a sailor at a disco. She liked him very much, but his ship has sailed away.*
Prediction: She won't see him again.
or
She'll never see him again.

1 Your friend Lisa is taking a mathematics exam this morning. Unfortunately she's not good at mathematics.
2 You have a terrible cold. Your friend hasn't caught it yet.
3 Your friend is in love with Tanya. He'd like to marry her, but Tanya's parents are rich and your friend is poor.
4 Alan is a very careless driver. He always drives too fast and he's had a number of minor accidents.

5 On two occasions recently Linda's boss has complained about the quality of her work. On the second occasion she was quite rude to him. Her boss is obviously becoming impatient.

6 The weather's been bad all this week, but next week Danny is going on holiday, and when Danny goes on holiday the sun always seems to shine.

7 Mrs Clifton often complains of pains in her chest, but her doctor has told her several times that there's nothing wrong with her. She's going to see him.

8 Robert is 16 years old and very forgetful. Ann has given him a letter to post. He has put the letter into his pocket.

NOTE HOW WE FORM THE SIMPLE FUTURE

Statements:

I'll (I shall/will) You'll (You will) He'll, She'll (He/She will) We'll (We shall/will) You'll (You will) They'll (They will)	see	her tomorrow.

Negatives:

I shan't/won't (I shall not/will not) You won't (You will not) He/She won't (He/She will not) We shan't/won't (We shall not/will not) You won't (You will not) They won't (They will not)	see	her today.

Questions:

Shall I Will you Will he/she Shall we Will you Will they	write	to her?

SPECIAL POINTS TO NOTE

We use the Simple Future:

a to make an offer or a promise.

▷ *Examples:* **I'll give you** *£200 for your old car.*
   I'll buy you *a watch for your birthday.*

b to make predictions.

▷ *Examples:* **He will be sorry** *he said that to his boss.*
   I'm sure she won't find *her key.*

c to announce a plan of action.

▷ *Examples:* *You stay here,* **I'll ring** *for an ambulance.*
   It's rather stuffy in here, **I'll open** *the window.*

d   to make formal announcements.

▷   *Examples:* *The Minister of Transport **will open** a new bridge over the River Seine this afternoon.*

*This evening the Prince and Princess **will attend** a special charity concert at the Opera House.*

F LISTENING

OPENING A BANK ACCOUNT

You are going to hear a radio advertisement aimed at young people leaving school. Before you listen to the tape, study the following vocabulary:

grant:	money given to students to pay some or all of their expenses
pocket money:	small amount of money given to a child each week
loan:	money that is borrowed (sometimes from a bank)
rate of interest:	amount charged or paid when money is borrowed or lent, usually expressed as a percentage (5%, 10%)
catch:	a hidden problem or obstacle
loyal:	faithful
suit:	be convenient

Listen to the tape several times if necessary and decide whether the statements below are true or false:

1 A bank paid for this advertisement.
2 Mary Green will start her first job in September.
3 Mary agrees that she will need a bank account.
4 Keith has already started work.
5 He earns quite a lot of money.
6 As soon as Keith opens a bank account he'll be able to borrow £200.

Write your answer to this question.
Explain briefly why the bank is keen to attract new customers, although they probably have very little money.

G WRITING ACTIVITY

Letter to a bank manager
Let's continue to think about money. Imagine you want to buy something quite large – a car, a boat, an expensive hi-fi system, perhaps.

Write a short letter to the Manager of the City Bank and ask for a loan.

Explain **why** you want the money and say **how much** you want to borrow. Then go on to say how much money you can afford to pay back each month.

Don't forget to put your own address and the date in the **top right hand corner** of your letter.

UNIT

17

▷ TIME FOR TREATMENT ◁

A WHAT KIND OF CLINIC IS THIS?

Reading

It was just four o'clock as Tony drove up and parked his Mercedes at the side of the fine, big house. He locked the car, took his leather suitcase from the boot and went in through the front door.

A slim, elegant woman, wearing a white coat stepped forward to meet him. 'I'm Mrs Zimmerman,' she announced. 'You must be Mr Coffey. Welcome. We've been expecting you.'

'Oh, yes. I asked my secretary to ring.'

Mrs Zimmerman nodded. 'I believe this is your first visit to the clinic.' She spoke quietly, but with an unmistakable air of authority. 'I'll show you your room and then you'd better come down to my office for a chat.'

The room was clean and bright and a white vase filled with yellow tulips stood on a table beside the window. Tony took off his blue suit and put on a green shirt, grey trousers and a yellow pullover. Then he went downstairs and knocked at the door of Mrs Zimmerman's office. She looked up from her desk and smiled at him coolly. 'Please sit down,' she said. 'We have a few simple rules here and I'd like to go over them with you.' Tony nodded.

'When you get your diet sheet, you must study it carefully and you mustn't eat or drink anything not on that sheet. Also you mustn't eat anything outside the meal times laid down by the clinic. You obviously need to lose quite a lot of weight, so apart from dieting, you ought to try and take as much exercise as possible.'

'Presumably we aren't allowed to leave the grounds?' asked Tony. 'No, you mustn't leave the grounds without permission from myself or Dr Bernstein,' replied Mrs Zimmerman. 'Now, I want you to strip down to your underclothes, I'm going to weigh you . . . no, you needn't take off your socks . . . right, stand on the scales, please . . . .'

UNIT

18

COMPREHENSION QUESTIONS

1 Do you think Tony is poor, or wealthy? Give reasons for your answer.
2 What can you say about Mrs Zimmerman?
3 Describe the clothes that Tony changed into.
4 Why do you think Tony has come to the clinic?
5 What did Mrs Zimmerman tell Tony he'd better do?
6 What did she tell him he must do?
7 What did she tell him he mustn't do? (Three things)
8 What did she tell him he needs to do?
9 What did she tell him he ought to do?
10 What did she tell him she wanted him to do?
11 What did she tell him he needn't do?
12 What can you say about Dr Bernstein?

B WORD BUILDING

Mrs Zimmerman told Tony to take as much exercise as possible. Of course, he could go **jogging**. Here are some more **ways of moving**.

Match each verb with the most suitable definition below and write in the past form:

crawl – creep – hop – hurry – limp – march – plod – stride – stroll – wander

Definition	Verb	Past form
1 walk as if one leg was shorter than the other	limp	limped
2 jump along on one leg only.		
3 walk in a military manner		
4 move around from place to place not quite knowing where you will arrive next		
5 move slowly on your hands and knees.		
6 walk slowly, as if your feet felt heavy		
7 move forward, slowly, silently and secretly		
8 walk forward with a definite purpose, taking large steps		
9 move quickly, as if you have no time to lose		
10 walk slowly, enjoying your walk		

C WORK IN PAIRS. DECIDE WHAT THE FOLLOWING PEOPLE _MUST DO_, OR _MUSTN'T DO_.

Example: A primary school teacher
   He/she must be _patient._
   He/she mustn't hit _the children, even when they're naughty._

1 Someone who works at a petrol station . . .
2 A postman . . .
3 A bus driver . . .
4 Someone who works at a zoo . . .
5 A ballet dancer . . .
6 Someone who works at a nuclear power station
. . .
7 A dentist . . .
8 A fashion model . . .
9 Someone who has had a heart attack . . .
10 A monk . . .

Exercise

D PAIR UP THE SENTENCES IN COLUMN A WITH THOSE IN COLUMN B TO MAKE TEN SENSIBLE DIALOGUES.

When you have done this, you will find that you have two responses left over. Think of suitable remarks with which to complete these last two dialogues.

Column A

1 She keeps complaining of headaches.

2 You needn't wash those dishes.

3 John and Mary aren't home yet.

4 Perhaps I'd better ring Jennie to make sure she knows the address.

5 I brought some sweets for the children.

6 I'm sure it was Stella who broke the teapot.

7 She's always short of money.

8 They're always complaining about the food in the canteen.

9 Say goodbye to Henry. He's leaving.

10 Your sister looks tired.

Column B

a You mustn't blame her for everything that goes wrong.

b Then I suppose we ought to take our umbrellas.

c I think she probably needs glasses.

d Why? Are you afraid I'm going to break them?

e She needs to find herself a job.

f Yes, I must go home, too.

g You ought not to spend so much money on them.

h She isn't coming.

i Yes, she ought not to work so hard.

j Yes, we really need to find a new cook.

k All right. I'd better leave on the light in the hall.

l Oh, then I needn't buy any.

E FINISH EACH OF THE FOLLOWING SENTENCES SO THAT IT MEANS THE SAME AS THE SENTENCE PRINTED BEFORE IT:

1 It's forbidden to swim in the river.
   You **mustn't**. . .
2 I advise you to telephone him first.
   You . . .
3 I have a spare ticket, so it isn't necessary for you to pay.
   You . . .
4 Why don't you take her some flowers?
   You . . .
5 It isn't a good idea to invite Frank.
   You . . .
6 It isn't necessary for you to wait any longer.
   You . . .
7 They don't allow you to wear jeans in that restaurant.
   You . . .
8 It's necessary for you to have a visa to visit the United States.
   You . . .

SPECIAL POINTS TO NOTE

must/mustn't

must can be an order or an instruction.

▷ *Examples:* **You must read** *your diet sheet carefully.*
         Passengers must cross *by the footbridge.*

mustn't is an order or a definite instruction.

▷ *Examples:* **You mustn't eat** *anything that's not on your diet sheet.*
         We mustn't cross *here, it's dangerous.*

need/needn't

to need means **to require**.

▷ *Examples:* *He obviously* **needs to lose** *weight.*
         This bike **needs oil.**

needn't means it isn't necessary.

▷ *Examples:* **You needn't take off** *your socks.*
         We needn't unpack *our suitcases until tomorrow.*

ought/should

had better — giving advice/suggestions
eg You'd better bring your passport with you.

UNIT
18

ought to/ought not to -(stronger meaning)

ought to/***ought not to*** has the same meaning as
should/***shouldn't***.

▷ Examples: **You really ought to take more exercise,** *you*
know.
She ought not to speak *to her mother like*
that.

had better

had better is useful for giving advice or making
suggestions.

▷ Examples: **You'd better** *bring your passport with you.*
I suppose we'd better ask *at the*
information desk.

F LISTENING

Listening

BODYBUILDING

You are going to hear a radio discussion about
bodybuilding. Before you listen to the tape, study the
following vocabulary:

bodybuilding:	improving your body (usually by doing exercises with weights)
run:	control
gym:	gymnasium (place where people do physical exercises)
huge:	very large
target:	something you aim at
develop:	make them grow larger
achieve:	gain, win
available:	obtainable

Listen to the discussion. Then answer the following
questions:

1 What does Bill do?
2 Why do people come to the gym?
3 What sort of people come to the gym?
4 What do the people who come to the gym actually
do there?
5 How does Lisa feel about women taking part in this
activity?
6 How does Bill respond to Lisa's point?
7 Listen to the tape again and make a note of one
occasion when the expression **mustn't** is used.
8 Listen to the tape again and make a note of one
occasion when **needn't** is used and one occasion
when **I'd better** is used.
9 Listen to the tape once more and make a note of
two occasions when **must** is used and two
occasions when **ought to** is used.

UNIT
18

G WRITING ACTIVITY

MUST/MUSTN'T

Imagine you work as an administrator in the clinic referred to in the text. You are asked to complete a short list of rules to be fixed on the wall in each visitor's room.

Write out the complete document. You may add any extra points you think necessary.

SUNSHINE HEALTH CLINIC

We want you to enjoy your stay at the Clinic, but for your own good we must ask you to observe the following simple rules:

1 You . . . (diet sheet)
2 You . . . (eat food)
3 You . . . (some exercise)
4 You . . . (weigh yourself)
5 You . . . (smoke)
6 You . . . (worry)
7 You . . . (relax)
8 You . . . (leave grounds)

Dr E Bernstein (Director)

UNIT
18

Reading

A FIND OUT WHAT COLLIDED — AND WHERE!

It was a beautiful Sunday morning and school teacher Donald Murray was flying his radio controlled model aeroplane near Beachy Head, a well known beauty spot in the south of England. The model had a wing span of over a metre.

Mr Murray, who built the model himself, from a kit, was using a hand held radio transmitter to control the model, when he suddenly noticed two hang gliders circling, some distance from his plane.

He at once manoeuvred his model round into a downward circuit and as he did so he suddenly became aware of a third hang glider, which was approaching from another direction. Within seconds the model collided with the hang glider, cutting through one of the support wires. The wings of the hang glider immediately folded and it crashed to the ground, causing serious injury to the pilot, Reginald Phipps.

Asked about the condition of his model aeroplane after the accident, Mr Murray said: 'Strangely enough the model wasn't badly damaged. But I've burnt it. I couldn't possibly fly it again, after that.'

Mr Phipps said: 'I don't blame Mr Murray in any way. It was just bad luck.'

COMPREHENSION QUESTIONS

1 What was Mr Murray doing at Beachy Head?
2 What was Mr Phipps doing there?
3 Explain the meaning of: **He built it himself, from a kit**.
4 What method was Mr Murray using to control the model?
5 What did Mr Murray see in the distance?
6 What action did he then take?
7 What happened next?
8 Whose fault do you think the accident was?
9 What did Mr Murray finally decide to do with the model?
10 Who did Mr Phipps blame for the accident?

Exercise

B WORD BUILDING

Fill in the crossword. Forms of all the words were used in the text.

CLUES

Across

2 A journey by aeroplane.
4 The person who flies an aeroplane.
6 A set of separate pieces from which something can be made.
7 Harmed.
9 Far away.
10 To run into something is to _____ with it.

Down

1 To hold up.
2 To bend.
3 The general line in which something is moving.
5 To send (message or electronic signal).
8 To be _____ of is to know.

C WE OFTEN USE THE PAST CONTINUOUS TOGETHER WITH THE SIMPLE PAST.

▷ Example: I **was opening** a tin of beans, when I **cut** my finger.
or
I **cut** my finger while I **was opening** a tin of beans.

Use the prompts below to make similar sentences.

1 Jim/cut/himself/shave
2 The light/go out/Mary/read
3 I/listen to/my new record/telephone/ring
4 Anna/check/the oil in her car/Tom/arrive
5 The guests/arrive/for the part/the news/come
6 Henry/make/a cake/they/turn off/the gas
7 They/make/good progress with the project/the money/run out
8 A dog/attack/poor Mr Frost/he/run/round the park
9 She/slip/on the soap/she/get out of/the bath
10 The baby/play/with his toys/the firemen/reach/him

D WORK IN PAIRS. MAKE 10 DIALOGUES BY COMBINING ONE REMARK FROM COLUMN 1 WITH ONE REMARK FROM COLUMN 2 AND ONE REMARK FROM COLUMN 3. USE EACH REMARK ONCE ONLY.

When you have completed your ten dialogues, you will have **two** extra remarks left over from Column 1. Add two more exchanges to each of these to complete the remaining dialogues.

COLUMN 1	COLUMN 2	COLUMN 3
1 He hurt his leg while he was skiing.	He said she was working too hard.	Yes, I believe so.
2 Why has he got his arm in a sling?	Yes, I was working with him in Saudi Arabia.	Is he going back?
3 What was he doing in Kenya?	Oh, she was there all right.	Yes, the pavements have been very slippery, haven't they?
4 What was she doing in Cairo?	Did it happen abroad?	Was that where she met Jim?
5 How was it that he didn't see the other car?	He was working on a coffee plantation, I believe.	Was he driving very fast?
6 Where did she lose her purse?		

7 What was he doing in Holland?

8 I didn't notice Sally.

9 What was Lisa doing?

10 Why was she crying?

11 Have you met Peter?

12 What did the Doctor say about Louise?

She was playing tennis with George.

She thinks it was while she was wandering round the market.

It had no lights.

She went there for a holiday.

He fell over on the ice.

Do you think she'll take any notice of him?

Oh, I didn't realise you knew one another.

I expect she was keeping an eye on Harry.

Is she any good?

It was bad luck, wasn't it?

Exercise

E YOU AND THE REST OF YOUR CLASS ARE STAYING AT A COUNTRY CLUB, WHERE MEMBERS CAN TAKE PART IN A VARIETY OF ACTIVITIES. YOU CAN:

— swim in the pool
— dance in the disco
— play tennis on the tennis court
— drink coffee in the coffee shop
— lie in the sun on the patio
— listen to music in the music room
— read in the reading room
— ride round the grounds on a horse
— work out in the gymnasium
          or just
— rest in your room

Suddenly a shot rings out and a famous actor falls to the ground, mortally wounded. Naturally the detectives wish to question everybody staying at the club.
Where were you and what were you doing when the shot was fired?

NOTE HOW WE FORM THE PAST CONTINUOUS

Statements:

I	was		
You	were	eating	scrambled eggs
He/She	was		
We/You/They	were		

UNIT
19

Negatives:

I	wasn't	
You	weren't	
He/She	wasn't	talking
We/You/They	weren't	

Questions:

Was	I		
Were	you		
Was	he/she	being	a nuisance?
Were	we/you/they		

SPECIAL POINTS TO NOTE

The **Past Continuous** is the tense we use to describe a past action that lasted for an extended period.

a   Sometimes several of these actions may occur together.

▷   *Example: It* **was getting** *light. The waves* **were breaking** *on the deserted beach and a grey haired man* **was walking** *his dog along the promenade.*

b   However the action or actions described using the **Past Continuous** *are nearly always interrupted by a verb in the* **Simple Past**.

▷   *Examples: The President* **was inspecting** *the guard of honour, when a shot* **rang out**.
The audience **were enjoying** *the film, when suddenly the screen* **went** *blank.*

F LISTENING

WHAT A CATCH!

You are going to hear Iris Evans interviewing Tommy Reilly, the Captain of a fishing boat, who had an unusual experience. Before you listen to the tape, study the following vocabulary:

skipper:	captain
crew:	sailors on the ship
mine:	kind of bomb that floats in the sea and explodes when it comes into contact with a ship
quota:	limit, amount you are allowed to catch
cod, plaice, sole:	types of fish
coastguards:	kind of coastal police force
vessel:	ship
blow up:	explode

Listen to the tape, several times if necessary, then answer the following questions:

1 Why did Tommy get a shock?
2 Where were they fishing?
3 Why weren't they fishing for cod?
4 Who first noticed the mine?
5 How did the mine get there?
6 What did Tommy do when they discovered the mine?
7 What happened next?
8 What were the crew doing when the navy vessel arrived?
9 What did the divers do? (two things)
10 What was Iris Evans happy about?

Listen again to the interview and make notes. Then work in pairs and tell the story of what happened.

G WRITING ACTIVITY

TELLING A STORY

Use the notes you made to write the story from the point of view of Tommy's son, Joe.
Begin like this:
We were fishing a few miles off Lowestoft, when . . .
You will need between 90 and 130 words.

UNIT
19

Reading

A DO THE ENGLISH POLICE USUALLY CARRY GUNS?
DO PEOPLE CARRY IDENTITY CARDS IN ENGLAND?

Paris was a different world from the small village where Mark and Janet lived. They spent a happy week there. They stayed in a small hotel on the Left bank, visited Montmartre and the Cathedral of Notre Dame, admired the paintings in the Louvre and wandered along in the moonlight beside the River Seine. Now they were back home, telling their friends Bob and Susie about their experiences.

'One thing I noticed,' said Mark, 'was the policemen. They all had guns. If our English policemen carried guns, I'm sure it would make their job easier.'

'Ah, yes,' said Susie, 'but if our policemen carried guns, then our criminals would carry guns too.'
'They often do now, don't they?' said Janet.
'No,' replied Susie, 'only a small percentage of English criminals use guns, even today.'

'I think it would make the English policeman's job easier, if English people carried identity cards,' suggested Susie.
'If they made us do that, it would be a restriction of the freedom of the individual,' said Mark, 'I think . . . '
'Restriction of freedom — rubbish,' interrupted Janet rather rudely. 'Susie's right. You'll say we shouldn't have driving licences next.'

'If the Government introduced identity cards here, some people would object,' said Bob thoughtfully, 'but they'd soon get used to the idea. Unfortunately real criminals would always be able to get hold of forged identity cards, if they wanted them. Do you remember, in **The Day of the Jackal**, how the hired assassin visited a graveyard and got himself a passport in the name of someone who died at the age of two?'

The other three nodded. 'Now then, who'd like another cup of coffee?' asked Janet.

COMPREHENSION QUESTIONS

1 Why did Mark and Janet go to Paris?
2 What sort of things did they do there?
3 What did Mark notice about French policemen?
4 What suggestion does he make regarding English policemen?
5 Susie doesn't agree. What does she think would be the result of this?
6 What alternative suggestion does Susie make?
7 Explain what Janet means by: 'You'll say we shouldn't have driving licences next.'
8 What does Bob think criminals would do if identity cards were introduced in Britain?
9 What's a hired assassin?
10 Have you seen **The day of the Jackal**? (If not, you should see it when you get the chance.)

DISCUSSION

Do policemen in your country carry guns?
Do you agree with Susie when she says that if English policemen carried guns, more criminals would carry guns? Why/why not?
What about identity cards? Do you have them in your country?
Do you think having to carry one interferes with one's personal freedom?
In England attitudes towards the police are mixed. Older people usually get on well with them, while younger people often criticise them. Why do you think this is?

B WORD BUILDING

Use the words below, which are all taken from the text, to form words that fit in the blank spaces:

▷ *Example:* **easier**   *These tablets will **ease** the pain.*

admired   1 I think that's an _____ solution.

assassin   2 They tried to _____ the President.

died   3 His _____ was never reported in the newspapers.

forged   4 The signature was definitely a _____.

hired   5 I'm _____ a car while mine is being repaired.

interrupted   6 The injury to Jones caused a short _____ in the game.

introduced   7 This will delay the _____ of the new tax for some time.

object	8 Susan's father has no _____ to Tom's taking her to the dance.
restriction	9 The seats are cheap but they offer a _____ view of the stage.
visited	10 Our _____ to the castle was very short, wasn't it?

C PRACTISE GIVING ADVICE.

Example: My torch isn't working.
   If I were you, **I'd put** *some new batteries in it.*

1 Goodness, I'm feeling sleepy.
2 My flat is terribly small.
3 I want to go somewhere really nice for my holiday this year.
4 Oh, dear, my car's beginning to get quite rusty.
5 My telephone keeps making strange clicking noises.
6 The food in the canteen where I work is awful.
7 The photographs I took at the party are really disappointing.
8 I'd like to go abroad next summer, but I'm a bit nervous about travelling on my own.
9 I can't read this small print. I wonder if I need glasses.
10 I'm so tired of cooking all my own food.

D BELOW ARE THE ANSWERS TO 10 QUESTIONS. WORK IN PAIRS AND THINK OF SUITABLE QUESTIONS.

Example: I'd see a dentist.
   Question: What would you do if you had toothache?

1 I'd see a doctor.
2 I'd find another job.
3 I'd drink tea.
4 I'd send for the fire brigade.
5 I'd buy another one.
6 I'd report it to the police.
7 I'd walk to work.
8 I'd try and take more exercise and go to bed later.
9 I'd write 'not known at this address' on the envelope and put it in the nearest postbox.
10 I'd ask them not to be so noisy, but if they took no notice, I'd look for another flat.

UNIT
20

Exercise

E THE SECOND CONDITIONAL IS USEFUL FOR MAKING EXCUSES, WHEN WE DON'T WANT TO DO THINGS.

▷ *Example: You don't want to play tennis.*
        Excuse: I'd play if I had a decent racket.

Make excuses:

1 You don't want to go shopping. (you're too busy)
2 You don't want to go on holiday. (you have no money)
3 You don't want to go to the party. (you're feeling sick)
4 You don't want to watch the film on the television. (the set's not working)
5 You don't want to take the medicine. (it makes you feel sleepy)
6 You don't want to go for a walk. (your shoes are too tight)
7 You don't want to make pancakes. (you have no eggs)
8 You don't want to ring her. (the telephone's not working)
9 You don't want to give him a lift. (your sister's using your car)
10 You don't want to lend her the money. (you don't have the key to the safe)

NOTE HOW WE FORM THE SECOND CONDITIONAL

Statements:

If	I you he/she we you they	spoke Spanish,	holidays there would be even more fun.

Negatives:

If	I you he/she we you they	didn't have a little holiday occasionally,	life would seem dreadfully boring.

Questions:

Would	I you he/she we you they	be better off	if we lived abroad?

SPECIAL POINTS TO NOTE

There are three conditional tenses, but the one we call the Second Conditional is particularly useful. We use it to talk about possible consequences things that might occur, as a result of other things happening.

▷ *Examples: English policemen don't normally carry guns. If they did, most criminals would carry them, too.*

Would there be so many murders in New York if it were more difficult to obtain a gun there?

The Second Conditional is also used for giving advice.

▷ *Example: If I were you, I'd resign from the club.*

*Note. You may hear: 'If I **was** you, . . . ', but usually 'If I **were** you, . . . ' sounds better.

The Second Conditional can also be used for making excuses, when you don't want to do things.

▷ *Example: For some reason you don't want to give him the key.*
I'd give you the key, if I had it.

F LISTENING

You are going to hear an extract from a radio programme dealing with listeners' questions about buying and selling property. Before you listen to the tape, study the following vocabulary:

finance:	money
house agent:	man or woman who assists people to buy or sell property
widow:	woman whose husband has died
Kuwait:	country in the Middle East
investment;	place to put your money (where you hope it may increase in value)
let:	allow someone to live there in return for rent
rent:	money you pay to live in a house or flat
lease:	legal document giving someone the right to occupy a property for a certain period

Listen to the tape, more than once, if necessary, then answer these questions:

1 What exactly is Mrs Rose's situation?
2 What information does Simon Smith ask her to give him?
3 He goes on to give her three separate pieces of advice. What are they?
4 Simon Smith also gives Mrs Rose two good reasons why he has given her the advice he has. What are those reasons?

UNIT
20

124

Writing

G WRITING ACTIVITY

GIVING ADVICE

You work for a magazine read by young people. It is your job to reply to letters from readers asking for advice.

A letter arrives from Paul Richard. Here is an extract:

> ... I am just 17 years old and I am having a difficult time with my parents. I am very keen on music. I have been playing the guitar with an amateur pop group for two years and I want to be a professional musician. My parents want me to stay at school until I am 18 and then train for some boring career ....

Reply, using not more than 120 words.

Test 4

1 WRITE FIVE QUESTIONS CONTAINING THE WORD 'WOULD'. YOU WILL FIND THE ANSWERS TO YOUR QUESTIONS BELOW.

▷ *Example:* To Australia.
Question: **If you could go** anywhere you liked for a holiday, **where would you go?**

1 I'd buy a new car.
2 I'd live in Rome.
3 I'd choose to be 25.
4 I'd start with grapefruit, then I'd have fresh bread rolls with butter and I'd drink coffee.
5 I'd learn to speak Russian.   10 Marks

2 OFFER A SOLUTION TO THE FOLLOWING PROBLEMS:

▷ *Example:* The house is on fire.
       You: I'll telephone the fire brigade.

1 Someone has stolen my diamond necklace.
2 Oh, goodness, I'm thirsty.
3 Bother, I've forgotten to bring any money.
4 I don't have a stamp and I want to post this letter.
5 Oh, dear there's someone at the door and my hands are all dirty.   5 Marks

UNIT
20

3 PUT VERBS IN THE FOLLOWING SENTENCES INTO THE SIMPLE PAST OR THE PAST CONTINUOUS:

1 While I (cook) the dinner, I (burn) my hands.
2 I'm afraid I (break) one of the glasses while I (wash) it.
3 The strange thing is that while I (sit) in a train travelling north, Jock (sit) in a train travelling south.
4 As soon as Nora (find) the photograph album, she (begin) to tear out all the photographs of Ted.
5 When Simon (wake up) the plane (come) in to land.

10 Marks

4 COMPLETE EACH OF THE FOLLOWING SENTENCES SO THAT IT MEANS THE SAME AS THE SENTENCE PRINTED BEFORE IT:

▷ Example: *It is necessary to show your passport.*
You must show your passport.

1 It is possible that I'll see you tomorrow.
 I . . .
2 It would be a good idea if you saw the dentist.
 You . . .
3 It isn't necessary to pay now.
 You . . .
4 It is against the rules to smoke in here.
 You . . .
5 There's a chance it will rain this afternoon.
 I think it . . .

5 Marks

5 CAN YOU IMAGINE HOW YOUR LIFE WOULD CHANGE IF YOU SUDDENLY BECAME FAMOUS? NOW YOU CAN WALK DOWN THE STREET AND NOBODY BOTHERS YOU OR TRIES TO TAKE YOUR PHOTOGRAPH. YOU CAN STILL BOOK A FLIGHT IN AN AEROPLANE, USING YOUR OWN NAME, BUT . . . JUST IMAGINE HOW DIFFERENT IT WOULD BE . . .

Write 100 – 150 words on: If I were famous . . .

20 Marks
Total Marks: 50

UNIT
20

IRREGULAR VERBS

Here is a list of the most useful irregular verbs.

be – was – been
beat – beat – beaten
become – became – become
begin – began – begun
bend – bent – bent
bite – bit – bitten
bleed – bled – bled
blow – blew – blown
break – broke – broken
bring – brought – brought
build – built – built
burn – burnt – burnt
burst – burst – burst
buy – bought – bought

catch – caught – caught
choose – chose – chosen
come – came – come
creep – crept – crept
cut – cut – cut

deal – dealt – dealt
dig – dug – dug
do – did – done
draw – drew – drawn
drink – drank – drunk
drive – drove – driven

eat – ate – eaten

fall – fell – fallen
feed – fed – fed
feel – felt – felt
fight – fought – fought
find – found – found
flee – fled – fled
fly – flew – flown
forget – forgot – forgotten
freeze – froze – frozen

get – got – got
give – gave – given
go – went – gone
grow – grew – grown

hang – hung – hung
(hanged – hanged for people.)
hear – heard – heard

hide – hid – hidden
hit – hit – hit
hold – held – held
hurt – hurt – hurt

keep – kept – kept
know – knew – known

learn – learnt – learnt
leave – left – left
lend – lent – lent
let – let – let
lie – lay – lain
lose – lost – lost

make – made – made
mean – meant – meant
meet – met – met

pay – paid – paid
put – put – put

read – read – read
ride – rode – ridden
ring – rang – rung
rise – rose – risen
run – ran – run

see – saw – seen
sell – sold – sold
send – sent – sent
shake – shook – shaken
shine – shone – shone
shoot – shot – shot
show – showed – shown
shut – shut – shut
sing – sang – sung
sink – sank – sunk
sit – sat – sat
sleep – slept – slept
slide – slid – slid
smell – smelt – smelt
speak – spoke – spoken
speed – sped – sped
spend – spent – spent
spill – spilt – spilt

spit – spat – spat
spread – spread – spread
stand – stood – stood
steal – stole – stolen
stick – stuck – stuck
swear – swore – sworn
sweep – swept – swept
swim – swam – swum
swing – swung – swung

take – took – taken
teach – taught – taught
tell – told – told
think – thought – thought
throw – threw – thrown

understand – understood –
understood

wake – woke – woken
wear – wore – worn
win – won – won
wind – wound – wound
write – wrote – written